Sailor

LeRoy Moore, Sr.

Sailor

A World War I Log

LeRoy Moore, Sr.

Transcribed by Jeanette M. Wiltse

Foreward by
Jeanette M. Wiltse

Epilogue by
Stephanie A. Wiltse

Cinema of the Mind
Starving Artists Workshop
Albany, New York

Printed by Starving Artists Workshop / www.cinemind.com
in the United States of America

ISBN: 978-0-6151-3475-8

October 2006

Dedicated to all those
who still go to sea
in defense of their country.
And all who continue
to serve their memories.

With special thanks to the present
and future crews
of the USS Slater,
the last Destroyer Escort
remaining afloat in the United States.
Now a historical museum moored
on the Hudson River
at our own sailor's home port
of Albany, New York
– right alongside where
Roy Moore used to canoe.

Table of Contents

List of Illustrations

Foreward

Registered Number 1747.

OFFICE OF THE
BOARD OF HEALTH
OF THE
TOWN OF CORTLANDT.
RECORD OF BIRTH.

Name of Child... LeRoy Moore

Place of Birth of Child... Peekskill, N. Y.

Date of Birth of Child... January 27, 1887.

Name of Father of Child... John William Moore

Name of Mother of Child... Jeanette Travis

I certify that the foregoing is a true statement of the birth of said... LeRoy Moore

... as recorded in this office.

Dated the 5th day of September 19 17.

Secretary.

My Dad, LeRoy Moore, was born to be a sailor.

When he was a boy he swam (without a boat) across the Hudson River at its widest point. His father's friend saw - or heard of - the exploit, and commented to Will "Chick" Moore, "I know your nickname is Chicky; I guess we'll have to call your boy Ducky!" (Ducky got a whipping).

LeRoy's father, John William (Will) Moore, a well-known master boat-builder and gunsmith (also, in later years, a stove-moulder) was a wiry, handsome man.

Will's beautiful wife, Jeanette Travis, died in 1890, when Roy was 3 and his brother Jesse was 6.

The boys went through more than a year in an orphanage, Vanderheyden Hall in Troy NY. They were then brought back to Peekskill where Jeanette's sister Alice Wood had agreed to help look after them. It was not a happy arrangement; Alice's son Ranny was favored over the Moore boys, in a situation straight out of "Tom Sawyer." They went to school, and stayed out of the way of Aunt Alice as much as possible the rest of the time. Accompanied by their dog Rex they spent their summer days in or on the river, swimming near their father's boathouse on

FOR SALE: This handsome launch, *Vixen II.*, 19½ x 4 ft. 8 in., 37 in. bow, 23 in. stern, cedar planking, copper fastened to oak frame, strongly built, no freak, lockered seats, finished in oak, workmanship the best, fittings nickeled, 2¾ White Star motor, nickeled head and pump pipes; can turn water in exhaust; is fastest or size on Hudson; perfect running order; no oars needed; new in June; used Sundays; kept housed; two sets Eastern batteries; has extra propeller; is really new; cost nearly $400; sell for $230. Owner wants larger boat; seen evenings or Sundays. Apply Launchman, 655 Highland Avenue, Peekskill, N. Y.

the Annsville Creek, or paddling a canoe he had built called 'The Mohawk,' in the shadow of the Storm King and the Dunderberg - the Hudson River Highlands.

Roy's brother, Jesse, migrated to the New York State capital at Albany when he came of age, fell in love with a vivacious dark-haired beauty named Lula Snider, and married her. He found work as a trolley-car conductor, then acquired a small truck and went into business for himself, as an iceman in the morning and an ashman in the afternoon. Known as the 'ashman artist,' his beautiful pastel landscapes of the Hudson Highlands earned a front-page spread in the Sunday Times-Union newspaper.

Roy Moore was a bright student, and a perfectionist. His high school record was a bright one; but he never graduated, having been so embarrassed by a mistake he'd made on his final exam that he walked out of school, never to return. He went home, bundled up some clothes and food, got on his bike and left. A week later, having slept in barns and haystacks, he was in Albany, where he found work and a home at the YMCA. He then got a job at the Albany Transit Company, working on the electrical gear atop the trolley cars. But his math skills and native fastidi-

U.S. BATTLESHIP NEW HAMPSHIRE.

ousness for detail made him a natural candidate for a better job at the General Electric Company in Schenectady. He moved there and found a new home, boarding with Richard and Mame Chrisler and their baby daughter Paula. He was happier there than he'd ever been.

Then duty - or adventure - or both - called. In 1908 he chose to continue his education at sea and was off to Portsmouth to sign on with the US Navy. He was assigned to the battleship New Hampshire as part of the 'electrical gang.' He "joined the Navy and saw the world," or much of it, with Teddy Roosevelt's "Great White Fleet," learning more of his trade, and

U.S.S. NEW HAMPSHIRE,

Navy Yard, Norfolk, Va.,

April 17th, 1911.

From: Lieutenant R.B.Coffey,U.S.N.,
To: The President of Examining Board.

Subject: Recommendation.

L.Moore,electrician 1st class,has served under me as electrician of No.2, 12-inch turret on board this ship, during the past year. He has performed his duties in a highly efficient and most satisfactory manner. There has not been a single casualty in the electrical gear of the turret during the year's firing of 118 shots from the turret.

I recommend him to the consideration of any officer who may have occasion to enquire into his past record.

R. B. Coffey

making new friends.

Roy's enlistment ended in 1912. He'd been keeping in touch with his father, sending postcards from every port, and went to visit him on his return to the States. He'd planned to sign up for another 4-year hitch in the Navy; but that didn't happen.

That visit 'Down Home' was a turning point. During the round of obligatory visits to relatives in Peekskill, Roy dropped in on his cousin Ranny Wood who worked as a coachman for the wealthy Huested family. As they chatted, a parlormaid appeared, with orders from Mr. H to hitch up the team, as he was going for a drive. Ranny introduced them and asked the upstairs maid to show the sailor out.

Their childhood feud long forgotten, Roy and Ranny developed a close friendship after that. Their visits increasingly included the

maid, Sevena Powell.

She was a slender, blue-eyed English girl, in the States only 2 years - a Lancashire lass from Barrow-in-Furness. Sevena had already been proposed to by a young man who wanted to take her away to California. She wasn't sure; she knew she'd miss her family. Then came Roy, the sailor home from the sea, handsome, cheerful, energetic, intelligent, and persuasive. Stanley Austin had to go to California by himself.

Roy had decided to settle in Albany where his brother Jess, now married with a baby son and daughter, was already established. He wanted Sevena to see the city before making a commitment, and accompanied her on an introductory visit to his brother's family. She liked what she saw of the state capital, and armed with a fine reference from the Huesteds, found work in the Madison Avenue mansion of the Staubs. In the spring of 1912, on a bench at the eastern tip of Albany's Washington Park lake, he proposed and was accepted, placing a simple diamond solitaire on Sevena's finger

ALBANY FURNISHES 45 MEN TO-DAY

Three Recruiting Stations Dispatch Men to Various Training Camps to Serve Their Country

Forty-five men were sent away to training camps to-day by the officers in charge of the local army, navy and marine corps recruiting stations. Of the number the navy sent away 27 men who had been recruited from time to time the past few weeks. The list included 20 apprentice seamen sent to Newport, five skilled mechanics to Brooklyn, and two former service men to Boston. The army sent away 11 men who were recruited to-day. Among them were two Albanians and one from Rensselaer. The marine corps station, Sergeant Edward P. Vadney in charge, sent away seven men. In addition to the 27 men sent away by Ensign Philip F. Hambsch at noon, eight men, including three Albanians, were enlisted and will be sent away to-morrow.

The recruits accepted and dispatched at the army recruiting station to-day by Captain Emil P. Laurson are: Albert J. Simmons, 134 Fourth avenue, Albany, infantry; John F. Dillon, 46 Morton avenue, Albany, field artillery; Patrick H. Lyman, 923 Broadway, Rensselaer, infantry; Arthur J. Penny, Liverpool, medical department; William F. Powers, Salem, infantry; Sylvester F. Cunningham, Waterford, medical department; Lewis S. Flower, Salem, field artillery; Stanley G. Judd, Cobleskill, field artillery; Howard L. Shuttleworth, Amsterdam, field artillery; Sherry E. Congdon, Florence, Vermont, infantry; Carl O. Abeel, Round Lake, medical department.

The men enlisted by Ensign Hambsch are: Frang G. Short, 215 Clinton avenue, Albany; Leroy Moore, 455 Bradford street, Albany; Melville K. Green, 600 Central avenue, Albany; Louis D. McLaughlin, Amsterdam; Christian Johnson, R. F. D. No. 2, Troy; Charles J. Dooney, Schenectady; Thomas D. J. Taylor, Schenectady, and Lewis Somm, Schenectady.

Sergeant E. L. Stark, in charge of the marine corps recruiting station, Humphrey building, 562 Broadway, has gone to the Catskills to spend a few days with his family. While he is absent Sergeant E. P. Vadney will conduct the office.

Boys between the ages of 12 and 18 years are eligible for membership in the local company of the American Junior Naval and Marine Scouts, which meets for drills on Tuesday nights in Beauman's academy, 119 State street. H. C. Edgerton, with offices from 2 until 4 o'clock p. m., 119 State street, is the principal promoter of the Marine Scouts in this locality.

They were married on October 26, 1912, in the rectory of a Peekskill church. A "shivaree," organized by Sevena's brother-in-law, followed them all the way to their honeymoon cottage (the old boathouse on Annsville Creek). Roy was annoyed, Sevena embarrassed by the loud revelry. But soon the noisy crowd was left behind, and the couple had a few days alone together before moving up-river to their first home, at 66 Lexington Ave. in Albany.

LeRoy Moore, Jr., made his first appearance the following summer. A happy, healthy baby, he was all the company Sevena needed during the long days when Roy Sr. was at work at the Circle Garage, maintaining the electrical systems on cars. But this happy interlude came to an end with World War I in 1917. Ever the patriotic American, Roy felt he had to re-enlist in the US Navy. He was 30 now, and slightly below the now-standard height for the service; but he secured a waiver. Friends tried to talk him out of it, since he was a family man with a very young child - but he was determined.

He found a flat in Peekskill for his wife and son, so they could be near his father and Sevena's sister Rosena. He put some of their furniture in storage and off he went to war. A man with experience now, he was given the rank of Chief Electrician on the Destroyer McCall. The "Mickey" crisscrossed the Atlantic between Portsmouth and Queenstown, escorting troopships, rescuing survivors of the deadly U-boat attacks. This book documents his first convoy on the "Mickey" from the pages of a very small journal, a few pictures and postcards, a letter and a poem.

LeRoy Moore, Sr. came home safely again in January 1919, when Sevena was, as she later described it in her Victorian English, "taken right away." In October 1919, I was born. Although he tried to re-enlist again during WW II, my father had returned for good to his family and to the river he loved.

– Jeanette Moore Wiltse

8/16/45

Jeanette Moore Wiltse and LeRoy Moore Sr
on the Hudson River at Albany, VJ day.

To My Wife

by LeRoy Moore, Sr.

Little you'd care what I laid at your feet

Ribbon or crest or shawl -

What if I bring you nothing, Sweet,

Nor maybe come home at all?

Ah, but you'll know, Brave Heart, you'll know

Two things I'll have kept to send:

Mine honor, for which you made me go,

And my love - my love to the end.

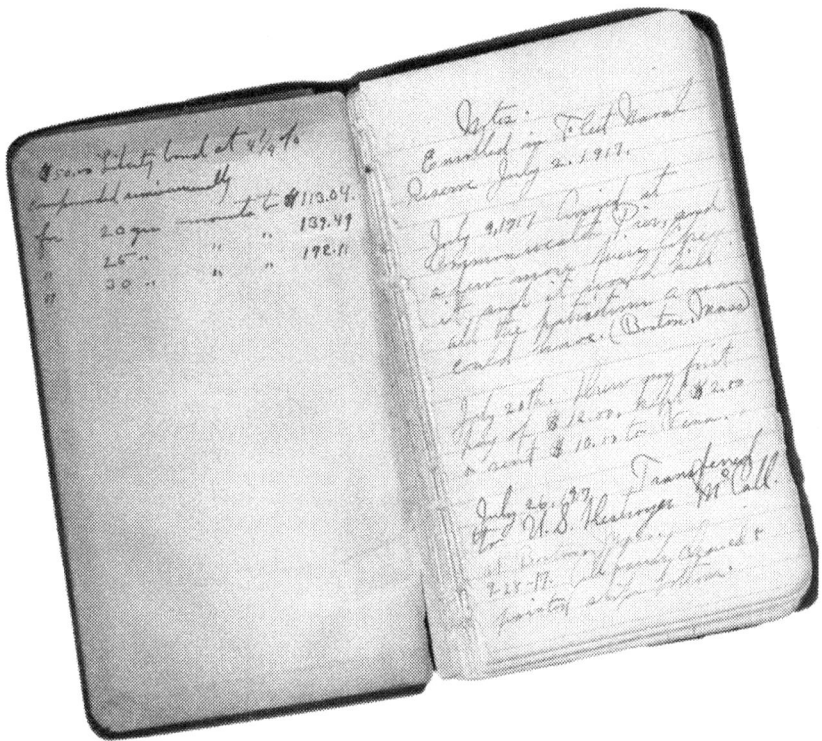

The World War I Log of LeRoy Moore, Sr.

Enrolled in the Fleet Naval Reserve July 2, 1917

July 9, 1917 Arrived at Commonwealth Pier, and a few more
---like it, and it would kill all the patriotism a man could have.
(Boston, Mass.)

July 20th Drew my first pay of $12.00, kept $2.00 and sent
$10.00 to Vena.

July 26, 1917 Transferred to US Destroyer McCall at Boston.

7/28/17 All --- cleaned and painted ship's bottom.

7/30/17 Tracing out line overhead to locate fuse box, walked into an open hatch, getting only a bum knee.

7/31/17 Started dock trial of engines about 11 p.m.

8/1/17 Dock trial, greater part of the day.

8/2/17 Engine test at sea from 8:30 a.m. to 3:45 p.m., returning to Boston Navy Yard, made as high as 29 knots.

8/3/17 Fixed up --- ---, don't know how long will last.

8/4/17 Wrote to Vena and also Ted. No news, just waiting orders.

8/5/17 Still awaiting orders. Wrote to Vena.

8/6/17 Had to hook up blinker lights on new yardarm. Rumored we leave tomorrow for the fleet.

8/7/17 Got under way about 10 a.m. for New York. Calm sea, speed about 20 knots. Dropped anchor and secured at midnight off Tompkinsville; plenty of ships of all kinds here. Passed a group of transports outward bound, convoyed by 2 destroyers and one cruiser.

8/8/17 Up anchor at about 11 a.m. in company with the New York, escorting her south. Sea getting rougher, speed 18 knots. Sea very rough by 10 o'clock. Had the 8--12 watch again on searchlight platform. We ran without lights; but New York had running lights.

8/9/17 Pulled in past the Cape early this morning, passed quite a few men-o-war, reached dock in Norfolk Navy Yard at about 10 a.m. to take on oil. Saw the new Mississippi and the Florida and Utah in the Yard. Finished a letter to Vena this morning.

Left the dock in Norfolk Navy Yard at about 11 a.m. for Yorktown, Va. on the York River and dropped anchor there at about 3
p.m. At time we anchored, there were about fourteen battleships,
four torpedo boats, and destroyers, besides several auxiliaries.
Wrote a letter each to Vena and Mr. Helliker, and also wrote one
to Ensign H--- concerning sending my Fleet Reserve pay to my
wife.

8/10/17 Had the ground trip to make today, delivering and receiving mail for the torpedo boats - but there was none for us. Left
Yorktown at about 9:15 p.m. to meet the President's yacht Mayflower, to escort it to the fleet.

8/11/17 Got up at 6:45 a.m., and found we had the Mayflower
about 400 yds. astern, having picked her up at 3:00 a.m. and
turned back for Yorktown. Came to anchor at 11:00 a.m. and
manned the rail as the President went by. Counted nine
dreadnaughts and seventeen pre-dreadnaughts besides auxiliaries.
Two --- --- at Norfolk. Up anchor at 4:00 p.m. and convoyed the
President, Woodow Wilson, and his yacht to Hampton Roads,
dropping anchor at 7:45 p.m.

8/12/17 Laying at anchor in Hampton Roads. Wrote one letter to
my wife and one to Mr. Hughes. Got up anchor at 3:45, escorted
the Mayflower to the mouth of the Potomac, left her there at 9:45,
and speeded up to 25 knots for New York - and are now returning
New York Harbor at 1:15 p.m. of the 13th.

8/13/17 Had the 4:00 to 8:00 a.m. watch this morning; calm sea,
and making 25 knots for New York. Pulling into harbor at 1:15
p.m. Went to Navy Yard, but was sent up to the North River
where we anchored at about 3:15 off 46th Street. They gave liberty, but not enough for me.

8/14/17 Laying in North River, liberty until midnight. Wrote to my wife, Mr. Hughes, and Jack Van Acker. Took on oil, water, and stores. Had to make mail trip; took L as far as Christopher St.

8/15/17 Still at anchor in North River. Rec'd pictures of my wife and boy. Made mail trip to Christopher St., down Christopher to Washington to Morton, and down Morton to West St. Rec'd letter from Mr. Helliker, sent letter to my father.

8/16/17 Left on mail trip, and had to report to the ship in the Navy Yard. Wrote to my wife, enclosing picture of the McCall.

8/17/17 Just waiting orders.

8/18/17 Wrote Vena and Roydie.

8/19/17 Went up to see Vena and Roydie at Nyack, N.Y.

8/20/17 Got back from Nyack on time, rec'd and answered a letter from Papa. Wrote Vena and Papa.

8/21/17 No news today, changed location "smoke bell and lights" in #1 fire room, some hot job. Rec'd letter from Vena and answered same.

8/22/17 Still at N.Y.

8/23/17 Left on liberty at 12:30 p.m., caught 1:14 train at Grand Central and went to Nyack to visit my wife and boy.

8/24/17 Got back on time this a.m. from Nyack on train (Erie R.R.) leaving Nyack at 4:58 a.m. Rec'd 25 plain post cards from Vena. Wrote post card to Vena.

8/25/17 Nothing new. Wrote to Mr. Helliker.

8/26/17 Went to see my wife and boy.

8/27/17 Returned to ship on time. No news. Sent a card to Vena.

8/28/17 Still in N.Y. yard, in company with the Balch, Terry, Roe, Worden, and a couple other destroyers. No news; nothing about pay either.

8/29/17 Rec'd letter from my wife, answered it, also wrote to Mr. and Mrs. Bateman and Harry Baldwin. No news, and still no pay.

8/30/17 Wrote my wife. No news.

8/31/17 "   "   "   ". The Duncan pulled in about 7 p.m.

9/1/17 Wrote my father to send birth certificate.

9/2/17 No news; got liberty at 10:00 a.m. and caught 11:00 train for Tarrytown, visited my wife and boy.

9/3/17 Returned on time. 3 destroyers have gone out: the Roe, Balch, and Terry.

9/4/17 Another destroyer in, think it's the Henly. We thought we were to sail today, but loaded on considerable stores. Henly gone out.

9/5/17 Rumored that some of us, including myself, whose accounts (?) are aboard were to be paid up to the 9/1/17, but this is 8:00 p.m., and no pay. But still in port, we still have hopes of pay.

9/6/17 Rec'd letter from Vena and answered same. Signed for and rec'd a pair boots, woolen socks, mittens, woolen jumper with hood attached, and two-piece waterproof suit. Inquired again about making an allotment, still nothing doing in that line. No news.

9/7/17 Rec'd letter from my father enclosing birth certificate. Left Navy Yard, N.Y. at 4:30 p.m., dropped anchor at Fort Hamilton and Wadsworth about 5:00 p.m., expect to get underway again at 8:30 p.m. I have the 8:00 to 12:00 searchlight watch; promises to be cold and rough. Sent post card to Vena before leaving Yard.

The Frederick du Gosse and another big transport put out to sea ahead of us. The destroyer Duncan --- near us. Got underway at 8:30 p.m., but could not tell how many ships with us. I had the 8:00 to 12:00 watch.

9/8/17 Sea getting rough. We have seven ships to convoy, and besides ourselves are the Duncan and the Huntington (armored cruiser, formerly the West Virginia). Got very rough about 4:00 p.m., carried away a range finder, a chest, and signal flag locker, denting our bridge --- ---; most of us seasick, myself included.

9/9/17 Still very rough; were compelled to slow down, so were left behind. Lockers in our compartment flooded. Towards evening, looked as though it would moderate, and increased speed to rejoin convoy.

9/10/17 Rejoined convoy about 1:00 p.m.; Princess Irene not with them. Was able to eat light breakfast; but ship is a mess both above and below decks - mostly below. Still a fair sea running, but not rough. Calmed down by midnight so turned in when I came off watch but almost went to sleep as soon as hit the bunk.

9/11/17 About 2:00, began to roll so you could hardly hang onto your bunk, as we must have changed course so that they were right on our beam; and it kept the anchor chains clanking so you couldn't sleep. But seas again calmed down by noon. Oiled ship about 3:00 p.m. off the Maumee, an oil and supply ship; we also got some fresh bread and meat from her. The former was very welcome, as our bread was becoming moldy. As soon as we got through and cut off from Maumee, the Duncan ran alongside her and also took oil and stores. The Maumee is partially disabled and cannot keep up with the fleet. Weather still nice, but getting cooler nights.

9/12/17 Wednesday. Good sleep from midnight to 7:00 a.m., just a long ground swell, ran back to the Maumee, took some more oil, all we could hold, and other stores, about 10:00 a.m., and left her, to rejoin the convoy. There are six big transports: the Frederick du Gosse, Baron de Kalb, Princess Irene, Mallory, Pasteur and Tendora. Ran into slight rain squalls about 11:00 p.m. Notice a stanchion in the ward room buckled from strain of Saturday's and Sunday's storm.

Transport – U.S. – World War 1.

9/13/17 Thursday - Back in position with convoy. Had to run alongside of Huntington, and her captain said we have to go 1800 miles yet on what fuel we have or else be towed. So they have passed the word that no fresh water will be issued us to wash in. Cold rain off and on at 10:00 p.m., looked like a bad night; but cleared and calmed down before midnight.

9/14/17 Friday - Fair day; changed formation to single column about 10:30 a.m. The Huntington leading the column, the Duncan off to the right of the head of column, and the Mickey to the left of the head of column. About 3:30 p.m. the Mallory cut loose with a few shots at something the Huntington was towing; and as near as we could see, she does good shooting. It brought our bunch up from below ready for action; but it was only practice. Had to rig dry batteries on two guns as the seas had washed over and filled the storage batteries, which are in a poor place on these boats.

Went on watch at 8:00 p.m. and could only make out one ship, and she acted more like a stranger; but guess she had trouble with steering gear, as she cut across our stern twice. They finally showed a signal which proved she was one of our bunch; she was still on our port quarter when I turned in at midnight.

9/15/17 Saturday - Up at six bells, and all the convoy in sight and just forming in column. The reason for us losing sight of them last night was that they had started the zigzag, as we are well within the sub zone. We were probably excused because of our shortage of fuel, and from a signal this morning it is evident that the zigzag is to be repeated tonight and tomorrow morning. The Frederick du Gosse, the deKalb and Tendora had target practice this a.m., and evidently can make it hot for sub periscopes if they see them in time. All ships have fired at practice, that is all of the transports. We dogged the watches tonight, I'll have the 4:00-8:00 for a week.

9/16/17 Sunday - Up on watch at 4:00 a.m., all ships in sight at 5:00, and went through a couple of zigzags until 7:00. We expect to meet some of our foreign service destroyers tomorrow sometime, then we will know for sure whether we are to go on, or back to the U.S.

Oil seems to be holding out alright; but we will get no fresh water to wash ourselves or our clothes in, till we connect with our Maumee. We are out of meat and bread, and also spuds, so guess we will get canned stuff for a few days. Supposed to meet our relief destroyers tomorrow at about 8:00 a.m.

9/17/17 Monday - Fairly good weather, slight wind and rainy squalls. Huntington had her observation balloon up early; and in attempting to haul it down in a wind storm, had it doing somersaults in the air and banging against the mast. Heard that one of the observers was seriously injured. No sign of our relief destroyers. At midnight, the most phosphorescent sea I ever saw, and the night as black as ink.

9/18/17 Tuesday - Made a tramp steamer heave to so we could question her at about 8:15 a.m. About 9:00 a.m. our relief destroyers began coming in from all directions, and at 9:15 we (the Huntington, and McCall) turned back for the States, our part of the job more than done as we took them more than a day farther than we were supposed to - and I guess that makes the tow line inevitable for us before we can reach the Maumee and oil. We had hard tack once already, and I liked it better than the flapjacks and biscuits we got. It will be hard on us to be towed in this heavy swell; but it sure has got to happen. Could not see how many destroyers relieved us but think six, as some say five and some say six.

We have seen nothing of a submarine since we started, but many a poor black fish coming up for a blow will never realize how near they came to getting a good wallop with a projectile for act-ing like a submarine. Sea getting rougher, and squall clouds threatening. Suppose we are in for a rough day tomorrow.

9/19/17 Wednesday - Rough, but sunny out. Huntington makes a pretty picture as she first buries her foc'stle and then part of her keel forward. Having a hard time writing this in heavy seas; and then we hit an extra large bump which almost jars me from the stool. At last, 11:30, we are on one end of a steel hawser, and the Huntington on the business end of it; also the sea getting very rough.

Re-fueling from U.S. Huntington.

Destroyer McCall - World War - Sept. 1917

9/20/17 Thursday - Getting rougher all the time. Am writing this by candle light as we shut down generators to save oil. Very rough, and very stuffy in my compartment, no blower running. We rec'd message from the Huntington, saying she had caught a message from the H.M.S. Cryptic saying that she had sighted a submarine yesterday in the same latitude and longitude we were relieved of our transporting, but guess the sub may have been there then and didn't want to take chances with 3 and 4 inch guns of eight torpedo boat destroyers and the 3, 6 and 8 inch on the

Huntington - not to speak of the guns on the transports them-selves.

Getting toward night, and seas calming down a bit; but signs of a blow off to our port - and we are only making 6 1/2 knots or 7 at the most.

9/21/17 Friday - Called at 4:00 a.m. to go on watch, and very near being thrown out of my bunk as soon as I sat up; and it is certainly rough and raining, also looks like it will be worse before the day is over. Still no wash; sure hope we meet the Maumee tomorrow as we are supposed to do. We will then have about six days' sail before we reach port. Still getting rougher.

9/22/17 Saturday - Got up at 4:00 a.m. to go on watch, and the seas are running higher than I have seen them so far, and wind getting even stronger.

About 6:30 a.m. the lookout on the Huntington sighted a ship, and sent the Duncan to investigate; and I was the first one on here to sight it at about 7:00 a.m., and it turned out

to be the much longed-for Maumee. And about 11:00 she was starting to oil the Duncan first, which makes it bad for us; as rough as it is, still getting rougher; although the sun is shining brightly, the wind is increasing.

The Duncan finished oiling about 2:30 p.m. and cast off. We cast off from the Huntington, having lit some more boilers - and after quite a little maneuvering got a tow line from the Maumee and another line with the oil hose fastened on it, and oiled slowly until about 4:00 p.m. when one extra heavy sea twisted the Maumee one way and almost threw us the other - which strain broke the towing hawser; and we had to cast off the oil line to save it.

We were still only about two-thirds filled - but would be dark by time we could get another start, so secured for the night. The Maumee going along with us, and will probably give us the rest tomorrow.

We dog the watch now, I having had the 4:00-8:00 p.m., and will have the 12:00-4:00 a.m. tomorrow.

9/23/17 Sunday - Bright star-lit night, and seas slightly moderated - but not enough to be elated over; toward morning, clouded over. About 8:00 a.m. were ordered to investigate a sailing ship, which turned out to be a French fishing boat - and we had a fellow in the crew who could talk French - so he soon proved to be right, and was allowed to go on his way.

It's about 10:30 a.m. and the Maumee is not in sight. At 2:30 p.m. we were ordered back to the Maumee to fill up; she was about 25 miles astern. Finished oiling, and rejoined the Huntington and Duncan about 11:00 p.m. Very rough night. If we have a real nice day on this trip, I won't know how to act. Still no water to wash in, and absolutely no excuse for it either, as we have more than enough oil to make port.

9/24/17 Monday - Still rough. About noon, sighted smoke of several ships on the horizon, eastward bound; we think it was another convoy - they passed northward of us. The Maumee will just about have time to get back to her station to oil the destroyers with them.

9/25/17 Tuesday - Still rough. We hope to make port Saturday or Sunday, which will be over three weeks at sea in an over-grown tomato can. They are going to serve us a quarter of a bucket of water today; I hope it will be enough for our hands. Getting smoother toward night - hope so anyway.

9/26/17 Wednesday - Was very smooth on the 12:00-4:00 a.m. watch, but just before 4:00 a.m. showed signs of doing stunts. And when I woke just before 6:00 a.m., it was because I was nearly thrown out of my bunk - and the rest of the time until 7:30 a.m., was just hanging on to the bunk.

After breakfast, went on top side and found that we were just maintaining speed enough for steerage way. Started to calm down on the 12:00-4:00 watch.

9/27/17 Thursday - Pretty nice day, no news. Speeded up at 2:30 p.m. to 14 knots. Intercepted a wireless from Arlington that a hurricane was headed this way, hope we miss the blamed thing. We have hopes of making port Sunday.

9/28/17 Friday - Still fine weather - must have missed the hurricane, and nobody sorry. About 8:00 a.m. a large steamer showed up on the horizon; and as it was on the Duncan's side, she was sent to investigate it. It must have taken her some distance as she (the Duncan) is just in sight coming up astern, and it is now about 11:30 a.m.

Served out another 1/2 bucket of water (I took a good half) out of which I got a tooth wash, a shave, and a bath. Had a heavy --- sea during night, but kept up a 15-knot speed.

9/29/17 Saturday - Had a very heavy wind and rain squall on the 12:00-4:00 a.m., and got drenched, but turned out to be a nice day after all. Speeded up to 17 knots about noon. Are sure we are going to Norfolk, Va. and it is some raw deal after the trip we have been on and the time our pay has been held up.

9/30/17 Sunday - Had the 12:00-4:00 a.m. watch; expect we will be in before noon so hope it's the last watch this trip. Could see land from deck at 7:30. Saw more ships underway than have seen in long time, about 40 British ships all going out, and about 10 of other nationalities. Wrote one short letter to my wife to relieve her anxiety as soon as possible.

Guess the English ships will go across in a bunch, under convoy of British men-of-war. Tied up to dock at 11:00 a.m. and preparing to oil ship. Our sides and decks are all rust-stained; one can easily see that we have had some rough weather.

10/1/17 Monday - Still had canned stuff. No news.

10/2/17 Tuesday - Busy day, went into dry dock. Read mail, a letter from my wife, Mrs. Hughes, Paula, Mrs. Chrisler, Mr. Helliker, and Harry Baldwin, also a knitted jersey from Paula.

We have a cracked plate on our bottom, and several other serious damages, including five or six hundred rivets loose.

10/3/17 Wednesday - Wrote letters to my Wife and Paula. No news, still in dock.

10/4/17 Thursday - Sent $150.00 to Vena, by postal money order, also registering the letter. Wrote to Mr. Helliker, also to my father. Very busy doing odd jobs.

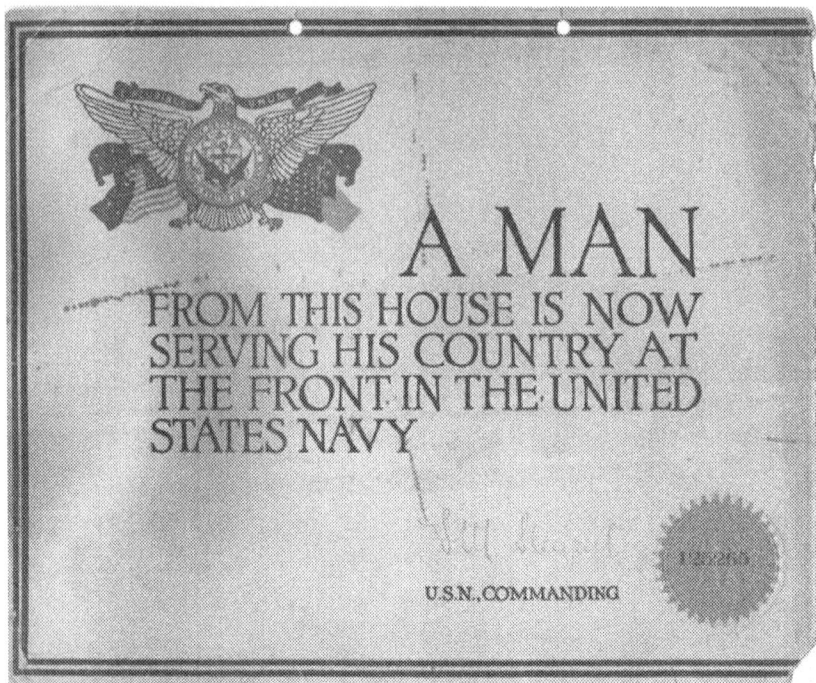

A MAN

FROM THIS HOUSE IS NOW
SERVING HIS COUNTRY AT
THE FRONT IN THE UNITED
STATES NAVY

U.S.N., COMMANDING

10/5/17 Friday - Wrote to Mr. and Mrs. Hughes, wrote also to Eliz. No news.

10/6/17 Saturday - Sent and rec'd answer to telegram to my wife.

10/7/17 Sunday - Wrote to Vena, also a special delivery. Rec'd a letter from her.

10/8/17 Monday - No news, still in dry dock. Asked for five days leave and was told to ask again tomorrow.

10/9/17 Tuesday - Granted 3 days and 18 hours leave. Rudd loaned me $15.00. Left ship at 4:00 p.m., had supper at the YMCA. Bought through ticket to NY, $8.25, boarded boat which left at 6:00 p.m. and landed us in Cape Charles in a little over two hours - where we boarded a New York, Philadelphia and Norfolk train; reached Jersey City about 7:50 next morning.

10/10/17 Wednesday - Reached Jersey City at 7:50 a.m., took Manhattan transfer to Grove St., had breakfast, and went to Erie station. Caught 10:01 train (a.m.) for Nyack, getting home by 11:45. Found all well.

10/11/17 Thursday - Visiting my Wife and Boy.

10/12/17 Friday - Visiting my Wife and Boy.

10/13/17 Saturday - Visiting my Wife and Boy until 6:16 train left for Jersey City. Made connections all right for return to ship.

10/14/17 Sunday - Got into Norfolk 11:30 a.m., over three hours late after a very disagreeable trip, old and crowded train. Paid Rudd his $15.00. Wrote to Vena and Roydie.

10/15/17 Monday - No news. Sent post cards to Elmer and George Bateman, Marie and John Hughes, Beatrice, Myrtle, Evelyn and Herbert Helliker. Filled out and turned in draft board papers. Also one to my brother, telling him not to sell my stove.

10/16/17 No news. Wrote Vena and Jess, telling him not to sell anything of mine. Sent cards to Ted and Dave, letter to S. Baldwin.

10/17/17 Wednesday - No news. Wrote my father a letter.

10/18/17 Thursday - Rec'd a letter from Paula. And later, one from Vena, answered same, addressing it in care of Mrs. Hughes.

10/19/17 Friday - No news, signed pay checks for half month's pay. Rec'd a letter from Vena.

10/20/17 Saturday - Paid today, rec'd $35.00 and sent $30.00 to Vena.

10/21/17 Sunday - No news. Wrote to Vena.

10/22/17 Monday - Rec'd letter from Vena. Put in to make a $55.00 allotment to her, giving Mrs. Hughes' address. The allotment will not reach her until January, but comes out of my December pay. Wrote to Mame and Dick.

10/23/17 Tuesday - No news. No mail.

10/24/17 Wednesday - No news, no mail.

10/25/17 Thursday - No news. One letter from Jess saying he had already sold the stove, before receiving my letter.

10/26/17 Friday - Rec'd Vena's letter of the 22nd. Rush work all day. Gave no idea when we will leave but expect soon. Vena rec'd $30.00 money order from me O.K.

10/27/17 Saturday - Moved over to oil dock, expect to leave tomorrow as they are only giving liberty until midnight. Wrote to Vena.

10/28/17 Sunday - Underway at 6:00 a.m. for the fleet at Yorktown, reaching there about 10:00 a.m.

10/29/17 Monday - Made one mail trip to the Paul Jones, but she had no mail for us, and late in the day was notified that I was relieved of the job - which was good news to me, and the only news of the day. Were to have gone out this morning to swing ship; but it rained and blowed a gale, so didn't go.

10/30/17 Tuesday - No news. Only eight big ships (all big-gun types) and five or six auxiliaries in here.

10/31/17 Wednesday - Had to go for mail again. Rec'd Vena's letter of the 25th. Rec'd message at 2:30 p.m. to get underway immediately to assist in some operation - presumably to look for the Michigan's lost launch, but not sure. Wrote a short letter to Vena. Came in after sundown without sighting anything. They say one body was found and one man living picked up by one ship.

11/1/17 Thursday - Rec'd a letter from Vena dated the 28th Oct.

11/2/17 Friday - No news. Rec'd two letters from Vena, answered same. In one letter Vena says she rec'd $11.00 from Jess on the stove.

11/3/17 Saturday - Underway at 7:00 a.m. Swung ship to test compasses, returned and anchored by noon. No news, no letter today - but didn't expect any.

11/4/17 Sunday - Rec'd Vena's letter of the 21st, and was like reading ancient history.

11/5/17 Monday - Rumor that we go across again pretty soon. In evening rec'd message to get under way, but was canceled. Four sub chasers came in and left again. Paid today, $33.00.

11/6/17 Tuesday - Under way at 6:00 a.m. in company with the Pennsylvania, Wyoming, North Dakota, and a big collier. Good weather to start with. Maneuvering all day, came back and dropped anchor in Lynnhaven Bay or Roads for the night.

11/7/17 Wednesday - Had the 12:00-4:00 a.m. watch. Under way at 6:00 a.m., maneuvered all day with part of the fleet. Were almost back in the Roads, and were ordered back to sea to inspect a floating object that had been sighted; and if it had been a mine we would be on the bottom now, as we hit it and cut it in two at 20 knots speed.

It was very rough all day, and promises to be a cold night. Rec'd two letters from Vena, dated Nov. 1st and Nov. 4th.

11/8/17 Thursday - Under way again at 6:30 a.m., maneuvering biggest part of the day with the fleet, returning about 3:00 p.m. and dropping anchor in Lynnhaven Bay - but were ordered to up anchor again about 5:00 p.m. and headed for Yorktown, Va., coming to anchor about 6:30 p.m.

11/9/17 Friday - No news; had to make the mail trip - rather, two trips, rec'd Vena's letter of the 6th. A bunch of us were caught with uncensored mail and reminded that it was a court-martial offense - so no more for mine.

11/10/17 Saturday - Under way about 1:30 p.m. for Norfolk to oil ship, reaching there around 5:00 p.m. Sighted about a dozen of our Naval hydro-aeroplanes in the air over Hampton Roads. Answered Vena's letters up to and including Nov. 6th.

11/11/17 Sunday - Under way at about 9:00 a.m., reached York-town and dropped anchor about noon. There are twenty-three battleships (including dreadnaughts and pre-dreadnaughts), three torpedo boats, one destroyer (ourself), the dispatch boat Dispatch, and two naval auxiliaries. Two more torpedo boats came in during the evening.

Made out insurance application for $5,000.00 to my wife, giving Mrs. Hughes' address. Also filled out application blank for Vena and Roydie family allowance of $40.00 per month.

11/12/17 Monday - Still at Yorktown. Our Captain (Stewart) left us today, may be going to London for some new duty. He was a very good Captain, and seemed deeply touched at leaving, and was given three rousing cheers.

11/13/17 Tuesday - My mistake: on this day our Captain left, and there was no news yesterday.

11/14/17 Wednesday - Rec'd Vena's letter of the 10th, Mame's of the 11th, and Harry Baldwin's of the 9th.

11/15/17 Thursday - Rec'd Vena's letter of the 12th, Paula's letter and a pair of wristers from her. Finished a letter to Vena. Vena acknowledged the receipt of my $30.00 money order sent about 11/7/17.

Underway about 3:30 p.m. at 20 knots, got into Norfolk around 7:00 p.m. in Hampton Roads.

11/16/17 Friday - Underway at 11:30 a.m. in company with the Wyoming, short choppy head sea, speed from 17 to 20 knots, sea calmed down about midnight.

11/17/17 Saturday - Had the 4:00 to 8:00 a.m. watch, at 7:15 a.m. turned around, leaving the Wyoming at the entrance of Ambrose channel, New York harbor, and started on our return trip; maintained a 20-knot speed all the way, and dropped anchor in Yorktown, Va. at 1:00 p.m.

11//18/17 Sunday - Oiled ship, and underway again about 3:45 p.m.; dropped anchor about 7:30 p.m. Wrote to Vena. Read Vena's letter of the 16th.

11/19/17 Monday - Under way at 6:00 a.m. with the entire fleet including 21 battleships, 8 torpedo boats and destroyers and 10 sub chasers which only went as far as Lynnhaven Bay with us. Very cold, and quite rough. Maneuvered all day, and it is said we keep this up for a week. We are headed south, and by midnight was getting warmer.

11/20/17 Tuesday - Started to rain at 3:45 a.m., much warmer, as we are getting into the Gulf Stream.

11/21/17 Wednesday - Very rough, in trough of seas. The Jewett, one of our sister ships, lost her fore-mast and part of her bridge at about 6:00 a.m. We lost one of our ventilators, and had our awning ripped up. We found our condenser leaking, salting (?) the water in the boilers. The Jewett started back about 8:00 a.m. and we started back about 10:00 a.m.

11/22/17 Thursday - Still very rough. Got out of Gulf Stream about 3:00 p.m. Called lookouts out of crow's nests in case our masts should go. We got into the Roads at midnight, where we anchored for the night.

11/23/17 Friday - Underway at 7:00 a.m., tied up at dock in Norfolk Yard at 7:45 a.m. The Florida left about 2:00 p.m., loaded down and camouflaged. Was given cheers by all present as it seems certain that she is bound for the other side. The rest of the 5th div. are going also, and include the Wyoming, Utah, Delaware and North Dakota.

Wrote short letter to Vena. Joe Tichnor came to inspect the submarine signal device, and he and I tested out all connections of same, and had quite a visit.

11/24/17 Saturday - The Paul Jones came in this morning, with her mainmast gone. Wrote Jess.

11/25/17 Sunday - Have heard that in order to get paid after this, we have to be in on the exact payday date, or else wait for the next payday; and such an arrangement may possibly extend our payday away back to the year 1890. Wrote short letter to Vena. Heard that the Jewett lost two men, the Pennsylvania and the Alabama each lost a man.

11/26/17 Monday - All hands called at 4:00 a.m., under way at 5:00, and anchored in Lynnhaven Roads at about 7:30 a.m. Up anchor again at 9:00 a.m., went out and maneuvered with the fleet all day in rough weather and very cold winds, coming back and dropping anchor in Lynnhaven Roads at 5:00 p.m.

11/27/17 Tuesday - Underway at 6:00 a.m. with fleet for maneuvers. Cold, but nice weather. Coming in about 4:00 p.m. escorting the Rhode Island (flagship) and 3 others of her type; and were almost in when the Nebraska, away in the rear, hoisted a breakdown pennant, and we had to go out again to escort her in. She apparently had one engine temporarily out of commission. We got in again about 5:30 p.m., dropping anchor at Lynnhaven Roads.

11/28/17 Wednesday - Up anchor at 6:00 a.m. for maneuvers; rainy and windy. Came in and tied up to dock at Norfolk Navy Yard at about 4:30 p.m. Gave 48 hours leave to 3rd section, and half of the 1st. We are to get our turkey dinner alright tomorrow. Wrote to Vena and Roydie, and to Paula.

11/29/17 Thursday - Thanksgiving Day - had a good dinner. Day somewhat overcast, and a little rain. No mail as yet, and no excuse for it. Had I the power, would certainly punish the ones responsible, especially as I think it is near here; and we are considered so little that they won't go to the little trouble to forward it to us. One doesn't mind a necessary inconvenience; but one doesn't like to be walked on either.

11/30/17 Friday - Paid today, rec'd $64.00, $3.50 having been taken out for insurance, though they have lost my application for same. Sent $60.00 by money order and registered letter. Rec'd

Vena's letter of the 25th and wrote to Mame, Dick and Paula. Our executive officer detached, and ordered to command the Hull.

12/1/17 Saturday - Rec'd 2 letters from Vena, 18th and 20th, and 1 from Mr. Helliker. Wrote to Vena.

12/2/17 Sunday - Was called up by executive officer and told that Mr. Haggart (who is going to command the Hull) wants me to go with him, and will make me chief if I go. Not all settled yet, but guess I'll go alright; don't like the looks of the Hull. We have orders to be at Lynnhaven Roads at 4:00 a.m.

12/3/17 Monday - Got under way at 2:15 a.m., anchored in Lynnhaven Rds. at 4:30 a.m. Under way again at 6:00 a.m. in company with the Hull, Pennsylvania, and South Carolina, staying with them while they fired their "big gun practice," and all turned back and anchored in Lynnhaven Roads about 3:00 p.m. The day had been calm and fairly cold.

12/4/17 Tuesday - Underway at 6:30 a.m. in company with the Arkansas, Michigan, and Hull. The two ships had practice, and we returned to Lynnhaven Rds. at 2:30 p.m.; nice weather.

12/5/17 Wednesday - Under way at 6:30 a.m. with the Pennsylvania, South Carolina, and Paul Jones. The South Seas fired almost all day We all tried out smoke screens, ours burnt up our stern light. My transfer papers to the Hull all made out, and Mr. Larsen told me I would leave tomorrow. Anchored in Yorktown with the fleet about 8:30 p.m.

12/6/17 Thursday - Underway at 6:00 a.m., anchored in the Roads (Hampton) about 7:30 a.m. Mr. Larsen told me I was going to stay on here for at least three weeks. I think we are going on another convoy trip. Rec'd Vena's letter of the 29th Nov. and 2nd Dec., also proofs of photos and registry receipt card. Under way again at 1:00 p.m. Cold and rough trip.

12/7/17 Friday - Reached Navy Yard New York at 6:30 a.m. and workmen started putting new wind shield on bridge.

12/8/17 Saturday - Had captain's inspection of the ship. Had 48 hours leave granted, left ship about 11:30 a.m. Left Grand Central at 11:04 p.m., reached Albany 5:20 p.m. Fare was $10.30.

12/9/17 Sunday - At Albany with my wife and boy.

12/10/17 Monday - Left Albany at 5:30 a.m., reached ship at 11:00 a.m., on time. Worked steady rest of day. Wrote Vena.

12/11/17 Tuesday - Worked all day, steady. Rec'd letters of Dec. 5-6 from Vena, and one from my father. Heard the very cheerful forecast of a woman prophet saying that the Mickey McCall will be torpedoed at 7:30 a.m. on Dec. 21st, 1917; so I'll be able to say whether she is as true a prophet as she is gloomy - that is if the Mickey is afloat after that date. It calls to mind Grubb's (a water tender in here) dismal dream that we will go down with all hands on her next trip, and he claims to be the 7th son of a 7th son. But as Vena is the 7th daughter of a 7th son, and cannot even foretell when I'll get my next pay (since I've been back in the service, I mean), I cannot say that I have any faith in his forecasting powers either; so will not lose much sleep on my coming trip except what I lose through standing watch, and hanging on to my bunk in rough weather.

12/12/17 Wednesday - Rec'd Vena's letter of Dec. 8th, and Papa's letter of the 10th; answered letters. Left dock at navy yard about 11:45 a.m., anchored at Tompkinsville about 12:30 p.m. Wrote Vena. Expect to leave at 10:30 p.m.

12/13/17 Thursday - Still here. Underway at 7:45 p.m., dropped anchor again in Gravesend Bay in a blinding snow and wind storm.

12/14/17 Friday - Rammed by two big merchant ships between 2:45 and 3:00 a.m. Sounded general alarm, all hands standing by their collision quarters. No one injured. We steamed back into the inner harbor and stopped quickly about 5:30 a.m. Decks and bulkhead between engine room and seamen's quarters all buckled up, and two big holes in our side. Took lots of water aft, but not enough to be dangerous. Was very exciting for a while, and fortunate it did not hit our depth mines. Got under way again at 7:30 a.m. and tied up at the dock about 9:30 a.m. Wrote to Vena.

Expect they will have a board of inquiry. I cannot see how anyone can be blamed, as the driving rain made it impossible to see the other ships until they were close aboard, and so many of them dragged anchors. It looked as though we were going to be crushed between a big merchant ship and the armored cruiser North Carolina.

We were ready to start on a convoy with the N.C. and the Terry, one of our sister ships, except she has three stacks instead of four. First section left on five days, second (including myself) are supposed to start on the 17th.

12/15/17 Saturday - Wrote my father. Left Navy Yard at 1:30 p.m. and went into Erie Basin floating dry dock about 7:00 p.m. (Brooklyn). Hooked up to dock juice at 8:30 p.m. getting only 75 volts to my switch board - which gives poor light from my 125 volt lamp equipment.

12/16/17 Sunday - Shipyard men started in on us, taking out damaged plates.

12/17/17 Monday - Wrote Vena I was going to see her. Still in dry dock.

12/18/17 Tuesday - No news.

12/19/17 Wednesday - Went to mast to get permission to start tomorrow and come back day after Xmas.

12/20/17 Thursday - Left ship about 9:00 a.m., reached Grand Central 10:15, just missing the 10:10. Went up on the 11:10 - but would have done better on the 12:10 p.m.

12/21-2-3-4-5/1917 - At home.

12/26/17 Wednesday - Left home at 6:30 a.m., caught 6:50 train, made good subway connections at Chambers Street for Brooklyn 4th Ave. line, reached ship on time at Sherman's shipyard.

12/27/17 Thursday - Wrote Vena. Moved us again after dark so had some more work with my telephone lead.

12/28/17 Friday - No news. Wrote Vena.

12/29/17 Saturday - No news.

12/30/17 Sunday -   "   "

12/31/17 Monday - Started on 48 hr. liberty, reaching home at 5:00 p.m., surprising everyone.

1/1/18 Tuesday - At home.

1/2/18 Wednesday - Left home at 6:30 a.m., due aboard at noon; but train late, did not get aboard until 3:00 p.m., but was excused.

1/3/18 Thursday - Notified to prepare for examination for chief electrician. No news.

1/4/18 Friday - Rec'd Vena's letter of 12/31/17. Wrote Vena and Roydie.

1/5/18 Saturday - Nothing of interest.

1/6/18 Sunday - Wrote to Vena.

1/7/18 Monday - Got 4 cakes soap off Seidle, owe him $.25 for same (PAID). Rec'd gloves from Vena.

1/8/18 Tuesday - Rec'd Vena's letters of 2nd and 3rd. Wrote Vena. Wrote to T.F. Carrier.

1/9/18 Wednesday - Rec'd Vena's letters of 6th and 7th.

1/10/18 Thursday - Rec'd Vena's letter of the 8th, answered same, and wrote to my father.

1/11/18 Friday - No news. Rec'd Vena's letter of the 8th.

1/12/18 Saturday - No news.

1/13/18 Sunday - Wrote Vena.

1/14/18 Monday - Rec'd Vena's letter of the 10th; wrote to her.

1/15/18 Tuesday - Left Erie Basin for Navy Yard, in tow.

1/16/18 Wednesday - Dock trial; expect to leave tomorrow. Bought and paid for 6 pictures, told Van Dyke of the Maumee to send them to my home address.

1/17/18 Thursday - Under way at about 2:00 p.m., outward bound. Put ice in ice box, so expect it will be warm where we are going. Fell off vaporator last night; have doubtful injury, but don't expect it to last long. Heard that our allotments did not go through. Struck something with starboard propellor so that it vibrates considerably; but captain decided to keep on.

1/18/18 Friday - Getting rough now.

1/19/18 Saturday - Very rough, expected to make port at 4:00 p.m. but did not sight the light until about midnight.

1/20/18 Sunday - Lay in the offing until 6:30 a.m., then took a pilot aboard, and steamed into harbor at Hamilton, Bermuda Island. Very pretty place, all houses and roofs are very white. Wrote Vena.

1/21/18 Monday - Still at Hamilton, Bermuda Isl. Had a steaming watch on from about 1:00 a.m. because of high winds, for fear of dragging anchor. Wrote my father about financial matters. Am so sick of this pay business that I don't care to make chief, or anything else.

1/22/18 Tuesday - Wrote Vena. Steaming watches on all night because of high wind.

1/23/18 Wednesday - Heard that allotments were sent to Philadelphia, Pa. and would probably go through in February or March. Mr. Williams told me of it. Steaming watch.

1/24/18 Thursday - No news.

1/25/18 Friday - No more liberty to be given here, because of a mix-up ashore, I suppose.

1/26/18 Saturday - Gave liberty. Moved down to the Naval Station. The Hopkins returned here, having lost her deck load of coal and one mast. The Paul Jones also returned, having caught fire during the storm; they say she is almost a wreck from it. They had started with some other coal-burners for the Azores. Also reported that two sub-chasers out of twenty-four that started, went down. The monitor Tonopah, and one of our L boats (sub) went out for a while today. The former yacht Isabel (now a pretty good torpedo boat destroyer) arrived early this a.m.

1/27/18 Sunday - News that one of our L boats was found with only three members of crew still living, after having been lost at sea for 38 days. We got underway at 11:30 a.m. to go to the assistance of a ship in distress, supposed to be about 300 miles out almost due east from the Bermudas. Sighted her at 11:30 p.m., after averaging about 20 knots. It was an American merchant ship, out of fuel oil (manned by a Navy crew); we gave her 7,000 gals. oil.

1/28/18 Monday - Finished oiling her, and left her at 5:45 a.m. and returned here at about 5:15 p.m. (Bermuda Isl.). Wrote Vena.

1/29/18 Tuesday - Oiled ship from HMS Caesar. Wrote Mame, Dick and Paula.

1/30/18 Wednesday - All hands, at 5:30 a.m. Cast off from HMS Caesar at 7:15 a.m., dropped pilot at 8:00 a.m., headed due east at 13 knot speed.

1/31/18 Thursday - Passed some ships at 1:00 a.m. Heard from an English ship having a mutiny; but was too far away for us. Increased speed to 15 knots at 1:30 a.m., decreased to 5 knots at 12:00 a.m. No sign of the other ships yet. Getting rough at 4:00 p.m.

2/1/18 Friday - Sighted smoke about 6:00 a.m., which turned out to be the repair ship Prometheus, the single turret monitor Tonopah, the US submarine L9, the torpedo boat Macdonough and a French submarine chaser. The Macdonough had target practice at 2:00 p.m. Speed since 8:00 a.m., about 8 knots. Fairly smooth.

2/2/18 Saturday - No news, smooth seas.

2/3/18 Sunday - Interned in dead fire-room with mumps. Sure is some place to be sick in.

2/4/18 Monday - No news.

2/5/18 Tuesday - Took in tow a disabled English trawler, which was in our course.

U.S.S. Tonopah on way to Azores. World War 1. (Mintler)

2/6/18 Wednesday - Oiled off the Prometheus.

2/7/18 Thursday - Trawler broke loose a couple of times, but we picked her up again; but were left behind by the rest of the group.

2/8/18 Friday - Caught up with bunch, and Prometheus took trawler in tow, attempted to tow us but hawser broke.

2/9/18 Saturday - In tow of Prometheus. About 10:30 a.m. was nearly thrown out of cot by collision between Tonopah and ourselves; slight damage done to our oil tanks.

2/10/18 Sunday - Still at sea, an awful night in fire room due to heavy roll, and condensed moisture dropping on me all night, so bad I couldn't sleep.

2/11/18 Monday - Isabel passed us, bound back over our course, to pick up our trawler which we had been compelled to drop, as we had no more hawsers. We are again under our own steam, but very little oil. Sighted land at about 8:00 a.m. and pulled into the harbor of Ponta Delgada, Azore Islands, about 2:00 p.m. Wrote Vena.

L. P., Brest - 7. BRIGNOGAN — Vue générale de la baie à marée haute, prise de la terrasse de villa Belle-Vue

2/12/18 Tuesday - Allowed back on the fantail about 3 hours, but was forbidden to let any of crew near me.

2/13/18 Wednesday - The Isabel came in with trawler. Besides ourselves, there is the gunboat Wheeling; Prometheus, Tonopah, submarine L9, the Survey and the Aristaeus, and another supply ship, besides 2 French sub chasers built in the USA. Took examination for chief, and was told I passed alright.

2/14/18 Thursday - Under way at noon with Prometheus and Macdonough, speed 14 to 15 knots, fairly heavy head sea for a few hours, but calmed down.

2/15/18 Friday - Still nice weather. Was told I made chief alright, certainly haven't been even asked an electrical question; was only questioned on A-N company drill, but was told that was all.

2/16/18 Saturday - No news. Fairly rough at night.

2/17/18 Sunday - Out of the fire room at last, go back to duty tomorrow.

2/18/18 Monday - In sight of land on port and starboard side, apparently the mouth of English Channel; we are being escorted by an old French torpedo boat, I suppose to guide us through mine fields. Clear and cold. Dropped anchor in the harbor of Brest, France, at 9:00 a.m. Sure is a rocky entrance to this harbor.

See a couple of our coal burners, the Stewart and Worden, also some converted yachts, and a couple of transports. About ten merchant ships headed out as we came in, two airplanes were flying over the entrance, and two big observation balloons up about a thousand ft. Wrote Vena.

We have about 15 destroyers here besides ourselves, eight of them being 742-tonners, but mostly coal burners. We have a hole or sprung plate below our water line where we hit the Tonopah; but it only fills our oil tank with water. Took on 40,000 gals. oil and pulled out at 10:30 p.m. with the Drayton, to find the Isabel and Macdonough, reported short of fuel. Heavy head sea.

2/19/18 Tuesday - Picked up the Isabel and Mac. Isabel had enough oil to get in by herself, so we hooked on to the Mac about

4:00 p.m., the Drayton and Isabel circling around us while we were getting our tow lines rigged.

2/20/18 Wednesday - Sighted lights off Brest about 1:30 a.m. Hawser parted at entrance to harbor at noon, so Drayton took the Mac in tow and we anchored behind breakwater about 2:00 p.m. The Drayton and Mac getting in about 3:00, the Mac giving us three cheers for bringing her in. She hadn't even steam enough for her steering engine, and was about out of fresh water.

2/21/18 Thursday - Mailed letter on ship for Vena. Got under way about noon. Got very rough. Had target practice and dropped a 300 lb. depth mine; and though it was set for 80 ft. depth, and though we were about 300 yds. away when it burst, it almost lifted her stern out of the water, and sent up a large amount of water.

Queenstown from the Water

2/22/18 Friday - Arrived in Queenstown, Ireland about 8:30 a.m. Rec'd mail, five letters from Vena, dated 1/16, 1/17, 1/19, 1/20, and 1/23/18.

2/23/18 Saturday - Several of our destroyers left today; we hear that six German destroyers got out; we are wondering if our bunch have gone after them. Wrote Vena, Papa and Jess.

2/24/18 Sunday - Posted on bulletin board, a bunch of advancements in rating, myself included as a chief electrician dating from Jan. 1, 1918. Wrote Vena and Roydie. The Downes got a sub last night with a depth charge, the bodies of three German sailors picked up on the beach.

2/25/18 Monday - No news.

2/26/18 Tuesday - About 24 of our destroyers in today. Our depth mine thrower being installed. Wrote Vena 2 letters. Told her to get me a Vol. 2 Bullard.

2/27/18 Wednesday - Oiled ship in morning, got underway at 1:00 p.m. in company with the Balch, Terry, Paulding, Jenkins and Patterson, making six of us, and an English Q boat and a small cruiser. Soon as clear of Queenstown we spread out as a fan, and made 20 knots. Quite rough.

2/28/18 Thursday - Very rough; sighted our convoy of 36 cargo ships, and took our positions on their outskirts. Very slow bunch, making between 6 and 7 knots.

3/1/18 Friday - Had general quarters about 3:30 a.m. and full speed through our convoy looking for a submarine a lookout reported; but there wasn't any so secured. Still rough and cold.

3/2/18 Saturday - Still rough. Convoy split up about 7:30 last night, leaving the Paulding and Mickey with only two ships to convoy; and the best speed of one of them is 7 knots. We have plenty of trouble with the fuel oil we got in Queenstown; it is hard to keep steam up. Sighted land about 10:00 a.m. and hope to soon be relieved of this --- convoy so we can head home to where?

Dropped convoy inside Eddystone Light for Devonport, Eng. and turned about with Paulding.

3/3/18 Sunday - Sighted land at about 6:15 a.m., tied up in Queenstown, Ireland about 8:45 a.m. Wrote Vena about her new religion.

3/4/18 Monday - No news; still in Queenstown.

3/5/18 Tuesday - One of our new destroyers, the Caldwell, came in. Wrote Vena.

3/6/18 Wednesday - No news, no mail (and no pay!!).

3/7/18 Thursday - Oiled ship at 1:15, lit off all boilers, went out to buoy. Under way at 2:15 p.m. in company with the Balch #50, Porter #59, Sampson #63, Ericsson #56, Jenkins #42, Terry #25, and McCall #28. Fairly rough.

3/8/18 Friday - Joined late in the evening by the Parker #48.

3/9/18 Saturday - Picked up convoy consisting of the armored cruiser Seattle, and 3 big liners with troops, at 8:30 a.m. The liners are the Agamemnon, America, and Mt. Vernon. Wrote Vena. Joined by the 36, #24, Monaghan #32, and the Warrington #30 about 3:00 p.m. Passed a westward-bound convoy (British) of 6 ships about 4:15 p.m. An American mission of some kind is on the Seattle, and the members must have their families along, as there are women aboard. Still extremely calm.

3/10/18 Sunday - Sec. of War Baker was on the Seattle. Still calm. Dense fog now and then. Joined by the Reid #21 about 10:00 a.m., making 12 destroyers - which indicates the importance of this convoy. It will sure have to be a smart and brave German that even takes a shot at one of this convoy, as all destroyers are zigzagging ahead, on both sides and astern of the convoy, and is more like combing than sweeping the ocean.

Pulled into Brest, France, at noon, and found out that we had escorted the Secretary of War in with us. Pulled out again at 3:00 p.m. with Nos. 50, 59, 63, 56, 42, 25, and 48 forming line abreast, thereby covering a lane over four miles wide for two of our big ships that are outward bound under escort of the Isabel, Roe and Reid; and the ocean is just like glass.

3/11/18 Monday - Beginning to wrinkle up a little, but not very rough. Reached Queenstown, Ire. at 3:30 p.m. Drew ten pounds - $48.69.

3/12/18 Tuesday - Rec'd mail, Vena's letters of Feb. 12 and 9th, one from my father dated Feb. 12. Wrote my father. Enclosed a check for $45.00 to Vena, check No. 142 from USS Dixie, dated Mar. 12, 1918.

3/13/18 Wednesday - No news. Registered letter with the check enclosed to Vena.

3/14/18 Thursday - Gunscamp, called Hetty Green, attempted suicide by cutting his throat, but may recover.

3/15/18 Friday - Read Vena's letters of the 15th, 17th and 18th saying she had rec'd a check for $35.00 from my father, also one for $30.00 from the Navy League.

3/16/18 Saturday - Under way at 8:00 a.m. with 7 others, speed about 12 knots.

3/17/18 Sunday - Fair weather. The Seattle and 3 destroyers passed us, the former being on her way home.

3/18/18 Monday - Sighted convoy about 10:30 a.m., consisting of the armored cruiser North Carolina and four transports, the former turned back to the States. There are 6 destroyers besides ourself: the Balch, Stockton, Porter, Jenkins, Sampson, and Ericsson.

3/19/18 Tuesday - Had GQ about 3 p.m., and one destroyer dropped depth charges; but we saw nothing. Convoy split up at 4:00 p.m.; two transports and four destroyers heading south - including the Drayton, which came out from Brest.

3/20/18 Wednesday - We - the Jenkins, Stockton, Ericsson and Mickey - with the other two transports, reached St. Nazaire about 9:00 a.m., turning back and heading for Queenstown.

Was repaired at end of war in British ship yard.

U.S.S. Manley - 1918- Explosion of Depth Mines
World War I.

38

We heard news of a disaster to the Manley, saying she had lost 71 men killed and a great many injured when 30 of her depth mines exploded.

3/21/18 Thursday - Reached Queenstown about 8:30 a.m. and oiled ship. Rec'd Vena's letter of Feb. 24th and Mrs. Chrisler's of Feb. 22nd. The Manley towed in at 6:00 p.m. with colors flying at signal yard, as her main mast was blown away by the explosion. Her builders deserve credit for the fact that her bulkheads held her up, as her hull from the main mast aft is just one mass of twisted steel and junk.

Answered Vena's letter.

3/22/18 Friday - Colors half-masted until noon, in honor of the Manley's dead.

3/23/18 Saturday - I increased my insurance to $10,000.00. Wrote Vena.

3/24/18 Sunday - Under way at 9:00 a.m. in a dense fog. Just missed a few collisions, and almost tangled up with the sub nets, but got out alright. Made about 20 knots, reached Bere Haven,

Ire. about 4:00 p.m., picked up our convoy of one 8-knot tank steamer, and headed out again. Fog lifted about 11:30 a.m.

3/25/18 Monday - Still going along Irish coast; passed Queenstown (our base) at 6:45 a.m. Making a wide zigzag all the time, which means we are lucky if we are making 7 knots along our base course. Pass any number of ships, but no subs.

3/26/18 Tuesday - Sighted submarine on surface about 6,000 yards off starboard beam at 6:15 a.m. Headed for her at full speed 31 knots, general quarters, and only held our fire as we had expected to sight an English sub last night; were about to fire, when she gave correct recognition signal, and guess next time she will be more prompt, or else will meet her finish. Got rid of our slow convoy, and turned almost at 20 knots (left convoy at Kingstown, Ire.). Wrote my father, also wrote Mame, Dick and Paula. Reached Queenstown at 7:00 p.m.

3/27/18 Wednesday - Wrote Vena. Rec'd Vena's of Mar. 1st, 4th and 8th.

3/28/18 Thursday - No news.

3/29/18 Friday - Wrote Vena. No news.

3/30/18 Saturday - Wrote Vena and Roydie. No news.

3/31/18 Sunday - Easter. Memories of last Easter take me back home with my Wife and Boy; but actualities have us standing by to get underway, which we did about 11:30 a.m. in company with four of our boats, one English torpedo-gunboat and an English Q boat. Queenstown is almost empty of torpedo boats, all but about four of ours having left during morning. Nearly slammed our stern against a "limie" merchant ship, and they say all hands on the "limie" beat it for the other end of their ship. I was unaware of it at the time as I was down in our store-room - where had the mines really got going, I would never have known what happened.

Fairly heavy head sea, slightly capped with whitecaps, but looks as though it will let up.

4/1/18 Monday - Joined convoy about 11:00 a.m. It consisted of 24 supply ships, whose best speed would be 8 knots.

4/2/18 Tuesday - Sighted another big convoy about 10:00 a.m. Were joined by 3 English destroyers about 10:30 a.m. Parted from the main convoy at 12:30 p.m. in company with the Q boat and the steamer Bushwood, speed about 7 knots, headed for Bristol, Eng.

4/3/18 Wednesday - Left our convoy at Bristol and turned about, and speed back up to 20.5 knots, for Queenstown, reaching there at 3:30 p.m. just in time to get out of a miserable storm which came up astern of us.

4/4/18 Thursday - No mail. Wrote Vena and Roydie. Drew 58# or $282.24.

4/5/18 Friday - Got a check for $225.00 to send Vena.

4/6/18 Saturday - Under way at 7:00 a.m. leaving part of our liberty party behind; rush orders. Sighted piece of driftwood, appeared to be a periscope, at 11:00 a.m., and another one at 1:00 p.m. At 3:30 p.m., came upon a splotch of oil; dropped two depth mines, and returned to the spot; and the oil was much thicker and deep down. Am personally certain we got a sub, but we have no proof. Sighted a lifeboat with three men in it at 3:45 and picked them up.

They were survivors of the Cyrene - and nine men who were with them in the boat died during last night. They were torpedoed at 7:00 p.m. yesterday off coast of Ireland. Continued our way. One

of the survivors said a British Q-boat circled around them but would not stop to pick them up for fear a sub would take a shot at them.

Arrived off entrance of the Mersey and picked up our convoy of 3 ships, the Teutonic, Adriatic and St. Paul.

April 7 Sunday - Left convoy at 1:00 p.m., reached Queenstown at 4:00 p.m.

April 8 Monday - Sent check #305 ($225.00) by registered mail to Vena, rec'd a letter from Roy Jr. Underway at 3:00 p.m. in company with the Wilkins #68, Winslow #53, Wainwright #62, and Ammen #35. Looks squally.

April 9 Tuesday - Very rough, making 15 knots, picked up the Aquitania about 5:30 p.m., loaded with troops. She lost us about midnight (we were leading the column) , though we burned a screened stern light for her. We made 20 knots - rough.

April 10 Wednesday - Calmed down slightly. Found our convoy again at 4:00 p.m.; left her off, Liverpool, at midnight.

April 11 Thursday - On the way back with Wainwright and Cummings, got in at 4:15 p.m. Wrote Vena and Roydie.

April 12 Friday - Under way at 11:15 a.m. in company with the Wainwright. Very smooth. Heard three explosions; finally came upon British Q-boat and she dropped another depth charge; we circled around at 25 knot speed and found nothing, so continued on our way. At 5:30 p.m. sighted one of our destroyers, head in opposite direction.

Wrote Dad, telling how my accounts stood up to April 1st.

April 13 Saturday - Anchored in roadstead at mouth of Mersey at 8:45 a.m. Wrote Harry Baldwin. Underway at 2:15 p.m. with Wainwright, Caldwell, Burrows and Beale, and 4 merchant ships.

April 14 Sunday - Were nearly rammed by one of our convoy about 1:00 a.m. Sighted the Balch and 5 more of our destroyers on their way back to our base at Queenstown, at 7:45 a.m. Heavy following seas; but as we are about four miles in advance of convoy and zigzagging across their course, we get some roll out of it. Wrote Vena and Roydie. Left convoy at 8:00 p.m.

April 15 Monday - Reached Queenstown at 1:00 a.m. Rec'd Vena's letters of Mar. 22 and 23rd saying she had given up pictures.

April 16 Tuesday - Wrote Vena and Roydie, reminded Vena of getting me a Bullard Vol. II.

April 17 Wednesday - No news.

April 18 Thursday - Signed up for a $50 Liberty Bond for Roy Jr. to be sent to Vena. Wrote Vena concerning same.

Underway at 11:45 a.m. with Wainwright, to patrol at 12.5 knots speed between Fastnet Light and Kinsale, about ? to ? miles. At

7:00 p.m. we rec'd wireless orders to investigate a sub reported 125 miles from our position, so speeded up to 25 knots, were about there when we rec'd orders to return to Queenstown.

April 19 Friday - Headed for Queenstown, speed 22 knots, were almost in sight of harbor entrance at 11:15 a.m. when rec'd orders to be at Holyhead, Eng. at 4:00 p.m.; so headed back at 27 knots, reaching there at 3:45 p.m. where we picked up a single ship speed 19 knots and took her to some place, only about 2 1/2 hour sail; turning back at 6:30 for Queenstown, speed 16 knots.

April 20 Saturday - Arrived at Queenstown at 7:30 a.m. Rec'd a letter from my father, rec'd my coat and trousers from tailor at Queenstown.

April 21 Sunday - Under way at 8:00 a.m. with Balch and Trippe. Smooth but cloudy. Wrote Vena and Roydie, enclosing program from the Army and Navy Club at Queenstown, Ireland. Increased speed at 12:15 p.m. to 25 knots, leaving Balch and Trippe behind, reached Holyhead at 5:45,

"Skinner's Monument," Holyhead

picked up 2 troop ships, taking them to Kingstown (near Dublin), arriving there at 8:30 p.m. Think these are Gurkha troops, to take care of the trouble in Dublin. Turned and headed for Liverpool.

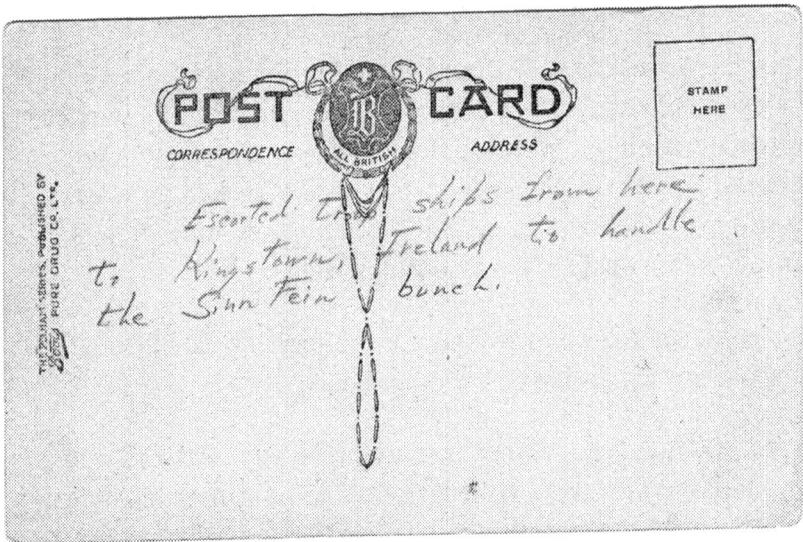

April 22 Monday - Arrived at Mersey River at 8:30 a.m., steaming across harbor entrance until 10:45 a.m. when our convoy came out - 11 ships and 4 other destroyers, the Allen, Balch, Jenkins and Trippe. Three air-ships (rigid type) went part way out with us; calm.

At 4:45 p.m., began to sight all kinds of wreckage including crates, wooden hatches, and hundreds of oranges from a steamer which had been very recently torpedoed; sighted what appeared to be a periscope on the off side of a life raft. Had general quarters and full speed; but was only the end of a timber sticking up.

April 23 Tuesday - Joined by the Wainwright and a double-ended craft. Early this morning barely missed being rammed by an English auxiliary cruiser, at 3:30 a.m. At 7:00 a.m., was awakened by several distant explosions, and the Allen was away astern after a sub which I believe she must have sunk as she fired three shots at it and then circled around the spot where it had submerged and dropped 14 depth charges, then took up her position with us again.

Wrote my father.

April 24 Wednesday - Dropped anchor in Bere Haven, Ireland at 9:45 a.m., having left our convoy at 1:40 a.m. Rec'd a wireless from the Cushing reporting a heavy oil spot where the Allen had dropped her mines, and stating she had also picked up wreckage from a sub - their having also dropped 4 depth mines to make sure; so Allen evidently got her sub alright.

Under way at 6:30 p.m. We have a submarine base in Bere Haven. We are with three of our other boats.

April 25 Thursday - Joined convoy of 34 ships at 10:15 a.m.; 5 of our destroyers and 2 British sloops. American merchant ships on outer flanks of convoy (note: all are American ships), probably because they are armed fore and aft. Calm and fairly warm, speed (zigzag) about 15 knots, convoy not zigzagging, making good about 8 knots.

April 26 Friday - Convoy split up about 10:00 a.m., 20 ships leaving us (in charge of some British and French torpedo boats) and 14 remaining with us (5 of our destroyers, including Mickey and an English sloop), bound for Brest.

Heavy fog; collision between the Westerly and another ship, the Westerly in sinking condition because her crew (a mixture of foreigners) started to abandon her right away.

We sent men over and they had to force the crew back on board at point of revolver. Also sent our collision mats over to her, and our men rigged them and secured things. They are now, at about 6:45 p.m., in tow of the British ship Camelin and they are holding their own as far as --- is concerned. Rest of convoy left us, the other ship having her bow turned over.

This incident shows the value of a Navy crew. Had her crew taken the proper steps, she would have been able to proceed under her own steam. We are about 79 miles from Brest. She is a new ship (Gov't built) on her first trip; her maiden voyage was her last. 8,000 ton capacity.

April 27 Saturday - Dense fog still. Westerly's crew again abandoned ship, which we found when their bell ceased its regular ring at intervals. They replied that ship was sinking, at 2:15 a.m. We lay off her port beam. The Camelin picked up her boats; no lives lost, we have her valuables and ship's papers. The Camelin had cast off tow line and was standing by also. Westerly finally sank stern first at 7:00 a.m. She was mainly loaded with flour. Three tugs were sent out to tow her in, but only one reached us just in time to see her sink. Still very dense fog; we are creeping along at about 4 knots. Increased speed to 14 knots to catch up with convoy. Sighted a sub in the fog; but fog closed again. War is certainly hell when you see your enemy and he doesn't see you, and a natural event like a fog hides him; especially rotten when you think he is trying to catch up with your own convoy.

Fog letting up at 5:30 p.m. - but as dense as they make them at 2:45 p.m. when we could have come to grips with a sub - but guess we'll get some of them before the war is over - if we don't get rammed by one of our ships or one of our Allies' ships. Now about 6:00 p.m., and we are speeding up to about 25 knots.

April 28 Sunday - Searching all night for a couple of ships lost during the fog, did not see them. Wrote Vena and Roydie. Reached Queenstown at 6:00 p.m. Rec'd mail, one letter from Vena, one from Harry Baldwin and one from Navy Disbursing officer saying I would get my Fleet Reserve pay when they get straightened out. Vena mentioned receiving a check from my father for $40.00, enclosed a pencil drawing of the Mickey from Roydie.

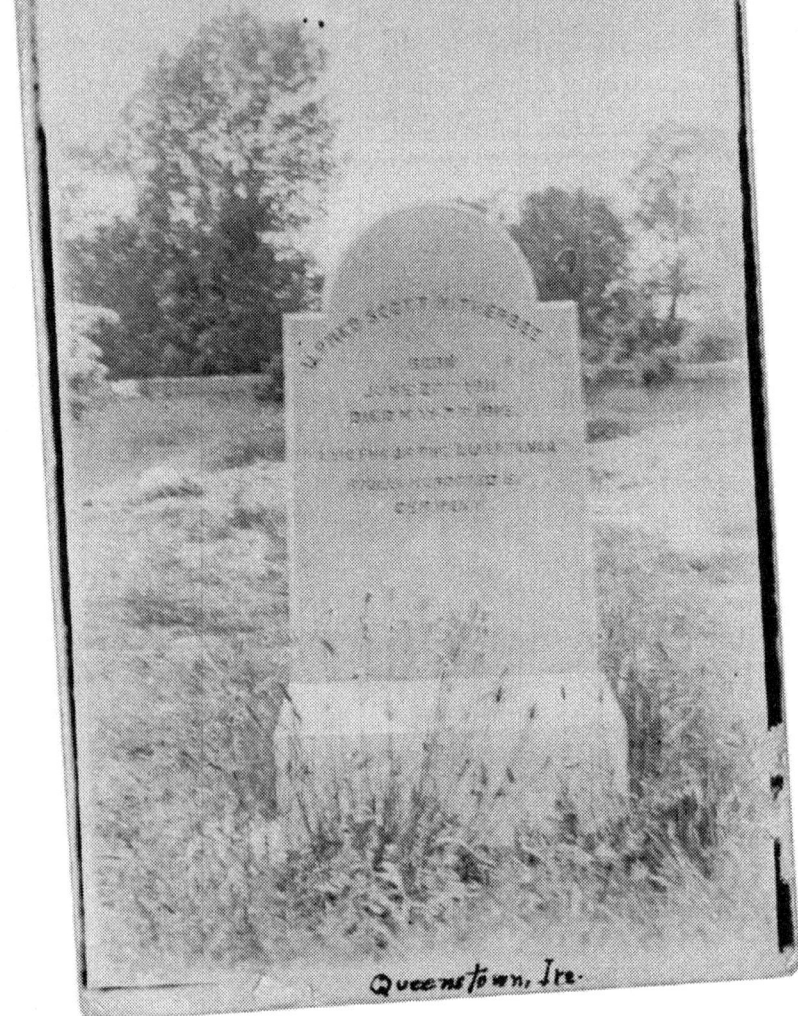

Drowned when Lusitania was
torpedoed in World War 1.

Queenstown, Ire.

April 29 Monday - Went ashore at 1:00 p.m., had a couple nice
walks - one out to cemetery where Lusitania victims are buried.
There are three big long graves, one about half as long, and two

littler ones, one containing two little children. The graves are kept in good condition by the Cunard Line.

April 30 Tuesday - The Cushing and the Allen have each got a sub during the past week, bringing evidence. The Allen is in dock getting her bow repaired, as she rammed and cut sub in half, then dropped two depth charges right on it. Other boats believe they got subs, but did not get any evidence to bring in.

Wrote Vena, enclosed picture of "Doc" and myself.

May 1 Wednesday - Wrote Jess.

May 2 Thursday - Wrote Vena. No news.

May 3 Friday - Had sailing orders, but postponed. Wrote Vena and Roydie.

May 4 Saturday - No news.

May 5 Sunday - Under way at 8:00 a.m. with the O'Brien. Sighted moving wake at 11:30 a.m. and dropped 9 "ash cans" on it; the general belief is that we got it, but no proof.

Depth Times - U.S.S. Fletcher - World War I.
Ash cans can be released from forward bridge.

May 6 Monday - Sighted Conyngham and the Cummings away astern of us at 6:00 a.m. Sighted convoy at 6:15 a.m., joined it about 6:45 a.m., 14 ships. Conyngham and Cummings joined us at 7:30 a.m. Convoy is all merchant ships. Admiral Beatty (British) complimented the "Mickey" for our attempt to save the Westerly. Also complimented all our boats, saying "It is an honor to command you and a pleasure to be with you; and to know you is to know all of the best traits of the Anglo-Saxon race." Joined by 5 British torpedo boats at 11:00 a.m. Convoy split up at 3:15 p.m., 8 ships going with British torpedo boats and 6 with us.

May 7 Tuesday - Lost convoy on 12-4 a.m. watch - foggy. Joined convoy at 5:15 p.m. At 7:00 p.m. the O'Brien which was at head of convoy sighted wake of sub, and dropped 19 ash cans on its wake, steamed back and dropped 2 more. Believe she must have got it; claims to have evidence. At about midnight, we took one ship from convoy.

May 8 Wednesday - Left ship at Holyhead at about 3:00 a.m., heading for Queenstown; but at noon were ordered to Liverpool to await orders; tied up to dock there at 2:00 p.m. Went ashore - was treated alright.

May 9 Thursday - Oiled at 10:00 a.m. Wrote Vena and Roydie. Underway at 11:45 a.m. with 3 of our destroyers and 4 big ships. At 1:45 p.m. we blew out a gasket on main steam line; ordered back to light ship; anchored and repaired, underway again at 5:15; speed 20 1/4 knots; at 7:00 p.m. increased speed to 25 knots. Very smooth. Rejoined convoy at 9:30 p.m.

May 10 Friday - No excitement, left convoy at 10:00 p.m. Changed course and formed scouting line with Cummings and Duncan, to pick up our other convoy.

May 11 Saturday - Joined our eastward bound convoy at 9:30 a.m. - 32 merchant ships and a cruiser. There are 7 of us and 1 British sloop. Fairly rough, but not bad.

May 12 Sunday - Little better weather. Joined by 6 British boats. About 10:30 a.m. one of our boats and a British boat began dropping depth charges, dropped about 20; don't know if they got it or not. About 2:00 p.m. Fanning dropped 4 cans on an oil slick; and one of merchant ships began firing at a vertical spar thinking it was a periscope.

Convoy split up at 3:45 p.m., 15 ships with British destroyers heading for Liverpool, and 17 heading for France, with 5 of our boats and 2 British sloops.

May 13 Monday - Took convoy into Brest, got oil off the Balch at 4:30 p.m., underway at 5:15 again.

May 14 Tuesday - Arrived Queenstown at 1:15 p.m. Rec'd mail, Vena's letters of April 5th, 8th, 10th, 16th and 21st; also Bullard Vol. II; Paula's letters of 11th and 22nd; Mame's of April 15th; and my father's of April 6th. Wrote Vena and Roydie, including another picture of Doc and I.

May 15th Wednesday - Wrote to Ted; wrote Paula; wrote Vena, special one ---.

May 16th Thursday - Rec'd Vena's letter of May 4th.

May 17th Friday - Wrote Vena and Roydie. Rec'd Vena's letters of Apr. 24 and 29 stating she had rec'd my check for $225.00. Went ashore, visited a real old castle and went through what is left of it Barrycourt Castle at Carrigtwohill, Ireland.

May 18th Saturday - Wrote Vena, also Roydie, enclosed a third picture of Doc and I. Underway at 5:00 p.m. with Fanning, Starrett, Cummings and Davis, and 3 British sloops.

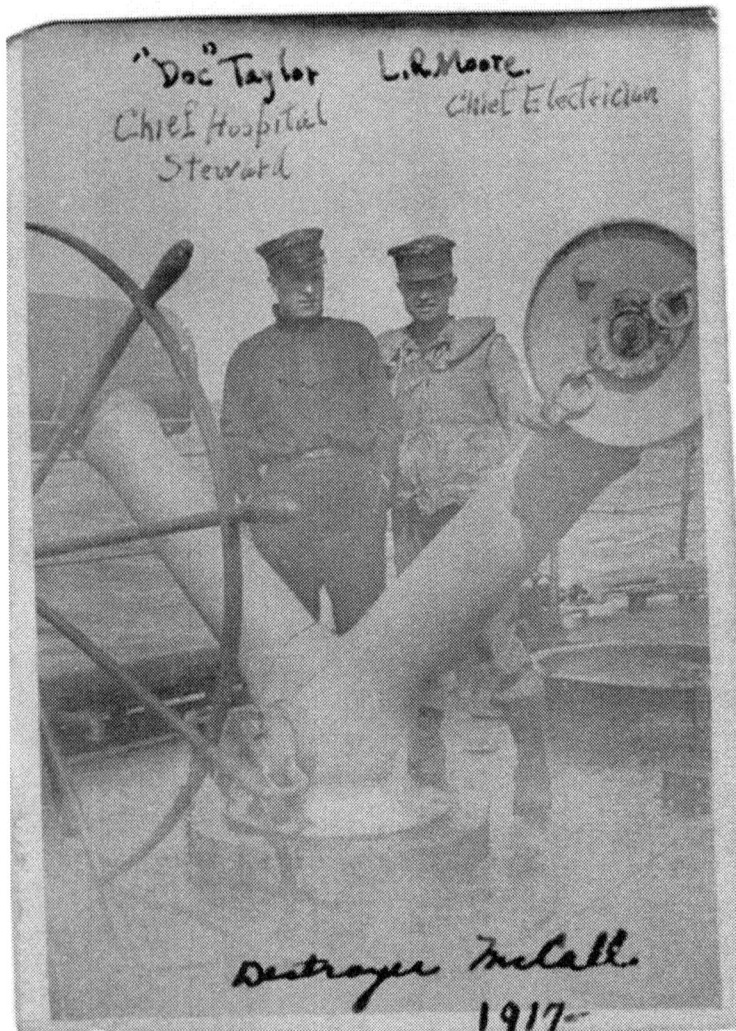

"Doc" Taylor   L. R. Moore.
Chief Hospital   Chief Electrician
Steward

Destroyer McCall
1917

May 19th Sunday - Joined convoy at 2 p.m., about 24 ships and an armored cruiser.

May 20th Monday - Fanning and Starrett left with 2 ships at 11:00 a.m. Davis dropped 19 charges on a wake. At 3:40 p.m., sighted 4 lifeboats from French steamer Metrone; British destroyer picked up one. At 4:00 p.m., British torpedo boat dropped 10 mines. Convoy split in half at 7:00 p.m., having been joined by about 8 British torpedo boats. One British boat and the Mickey convoying the British cruiser at about 22 knot speed.

May 21st Tuesday - Arrived Devonport 4:00 a.m., left at 4:30 a.m. with slow merchant ship and 1 British torpedo boat. Saw wake in fog --- at 2:00 p.m., gave chase; turned out to be a British sub chaser. Calm weather.

May 22nd Wednesday - Arrived Queenstown 11:45 a.m. Wrote Vena and Roydie.

May 23rd Thursday - No news.

May 24th Friday - Wrote Mame and Dick. Drew small --- $8.98. Under way at 2:00 p.m. with cable ship Farsley, 1 sloop and 2 drifters, speed about 8 knots. Choppy.

May 25th Saturday - Left convoy at 11:00 p.m. to aid ship which called for help.

May 26th Sunday - Sighted steamer Rathlin Head, Belfast - was torpedoed last night and twice this a.m. Tried out sub detector, dropped 11 charges; last one apparently took effect, but have no evidence to bring back. Two tugs came out, got her in tow about 2:00 p.m.; she has a bad list to port. Think we got sub, not sure, circling around tugs and steamer, making about 4 knots good; we are circling at about 16 knots. Have about 15 of her crew, tugs have rest, except 4 dead.

May 27th Monday - Joined by drifter which has a line on stern of steamer, holding her even to a line with tugs.

Wrote Vena and Roydie, told Vena to send me Bullard's Vol. I, Theory. Got into Bere Haven about 9:00 p.m. with our "wreck." She was trailing 150 fathoms of anchor chain, one torpedo having knocked the bottom out of her chain locker. The captain of the Rathlin Head gave us the pleasant news that 5 torpedoes were seen heading for the Mickey; well, if they don't come any closer than that, we should worry; as none of us even saw one of them - but don't think the same sub will fire any more, as another explosion followed the explosion of the last depth charge we dropped.

Oiled ship, and Rathlin Head's crew returned to her.

5/28th Tuesday - Under way at 2:30 p.m., arrived Queenstown 8:00 p.m., oiled ship. Rec'd letter from Harry Baldwin.

May 29th Wednesday - Wrote H. Baldwin, Dad, and Vena and Roydie. Dixie rec'd report that a steamer picked up bodies of 3 Germans where we dropped depth charges, bearing out statements of several of our crew who claimed to have heard a second muffled explosion following that of our last depth charge.

May 30th Thursday - No news.

May 31st Friday - Under way 8:00 a.m. with Starrett and an oil tanker. At 6:00 p.m. Starrett sighted oil slick and left to drop mines; had not rejoined at midnight; we kept on with our convoy.

June 1st Saturday - Had radio from Starrett about 8:00 a.m. indicated she had damaged sub, but apparently had used all her depth charges; is following oil slick in hopes sub will come to surface. Boatswain reported a torpedo passed 50 yds. from our stern about 8:00 p.m.; but guess he was mistaken.

June 2nd Sunday - Joined convoy 3:30 p.m., 15 ships and 5 destroyers. The Terry and one of merchant ships dropped charges on oil slick 9:00 p.m.; don't know if any results.

June 3rd Monday - Left convoy at 12:30 a.m. as we are almost out of oil.

Wrote Vena and Roydie. Rec'd Vena's letter of May 7th, and check for $37.35 Fleet Reserve pay. Ans'd Vena's letter. Arrived

Queenstown 11:30 a.m., left again at 3:00 p.m. Crew were paid; not I - two months since I was paid. Rejoined convoy about 9:00 p.m.

June 4th Tuesday - Sighted oil slick. Terry, Cushing and ourselves stayed back; Terry dropped 2 charges at 1:00 p.m. Ordered to rejoin convoy at 3:00 p.m., reached Liverpool at 4:30 p.m. Went ashore at 6:00 p.m.

June 5th Wednesday - Returned aboard 1:00 a.m., under way at 6:00 a.m. 8 ships and 6 destroyers, the Wilkes, Ericsson, Cushing, Terry, Starrett and Mickey. Foggy; at 4:30 p.m. Wilkes dropped couple of charges on a wake.

June 6th Thursday - Got fairly rough at 3:00 p.m. Terry ordered back to Base 6. We were ordered back at 10:00 p.m.

June 7th Thursday - Arrived Queenstown 9:00 a.m. The Mickey is in imperative need of overhauling, and has been for some time. The rotors of our main turbines are almost down on the casings.

June 8th Friday - Rec'd letter from my father, enclosing one from Aunt Eva; answered both.

June 9th Saturday - Wrote Vena and Roydie. Under way at 11:30 a.m. with tanker and trawler. Rough, and then some. Steering gear jammed twice on 8-12 p.m. watch.

June 10th Sunday - Fire-room went on the bum about 2:00 a.m., got started again at 8:45 a.m. Some bait for subs, but none took a shot at us - and we got some banging around by seas. Made 20 knots head on into seas, made Liverpool at 9:00 p.m.

June 11th Monday - Went into Cammell Laird Ship Co's. basin at 11:00 a.m. (Liverpool). Went ashore, cashed check (fleet reserve), getting full value at Wells Fargo express office.

June 12th Tuesday - Shipyard men started work. Stockton went out at 1:00 p.m. Wrote Vena and Roydie.

June 13th Wednesday - Went to Royal Theatre in Birkenhead. Not much good.

June 14th Thursday - No news.

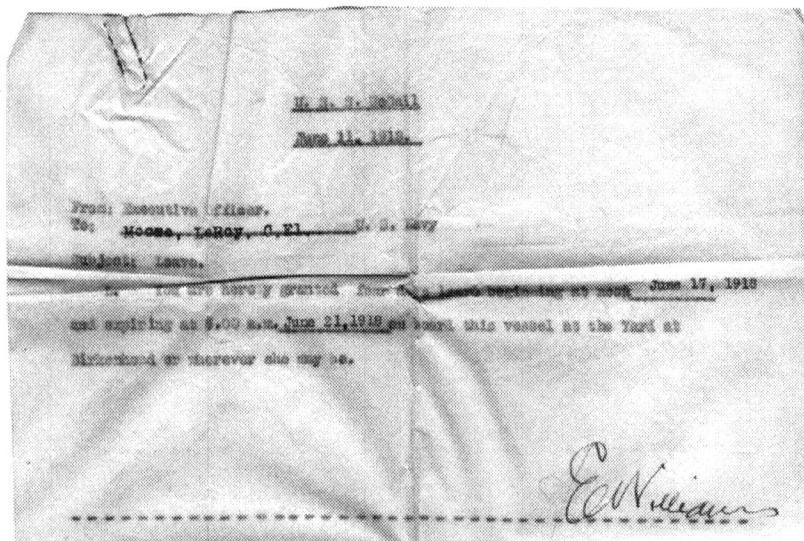

June 15th Friday - Went ashore early. Saw the Army team beat our team 6-2 at baseball at Goodison Park, Liverpool. Went to the Argyle Theatre, Birkenhead.

June 16th Saturday - Wrote Vena. No news.

June 17th Sunday - Started on leave. Reached Barrow-in-Furness about 6:00 p.m.; visited Vena's old home, found address of her Aunt Margaret (Burrow), Chapel St., Dalton-in-Furness, and was soon there (going by auto bus) and was warmly welcomed and pressed to stay there with Aunt Margaret and her daughter Belle.

June 18th Monday - Visited Furness Abbey with Aunt Margaret in the afternoon, and later in the afternoon and evening visited with more of the family out in the country. Was very well entertained by all, and by Belle especially, during the walk out and back.

June 19th Tuesday - Not very good day, so didn't go far; but cleared up in evening, and Belle and I went to Barrow and Walney, walking part of the way.

June 20th Wednesday - Stayed in most of the day, leaving Dalton on the 8:25 p.m., Belle and Aunt Margaret seeing me off. Changed at Carnforth, also at Prestwick.

June 21st Thursday - Arrived Liverpool at 12:45 a.m. Back on ship at Cammell-Laird's at 1:00 a.m. Wrote Aunt Margaret and Belle. Wrote Vena and Roydie.

June 22nd Friday - Had picture taken on Lord St., Liverpool, to be sent home. Paid for same, one dollar.

June 23rd Saturday - Wrote Vena and Roydie.

June 24th Sunday - Rec'd Vena and Roydie's letters of May 17th and 21st, answered same.

M. 41.

SPECIAL EMERGENCY CARD, SOLDIER OR SAILOR.

1. Holder—
(Name and Number) .... Moore, Leroy ....

2. Unit or Ship .... U.S.S.McCall ....

3. Proceeding from .... Liverpool .... to ....

4. Beginning of leave or duty .... June 17, 1918 ....

5. End of leave or duty .... June 21, 1918 ....

6. Is holder proceeding at end of leave or duty on Active Service or Service afloat? .... Service afloat ....

7. Signature of Officer issuing ....

8. Unit or Ship of Officer issuing .... U.S.S.McCall ....

INSTRUCTIONS TO HOLDER.

1. Each butter and margarine coupon represents one week's civilian ration. The meat coupons entitle you to purchase meat at a shop according to the official Table of Equivalent Weights displayed in the shop. Coupons marked "Other Meat Only" cannot be used to buy butcher's meat or pork. A coupon or half-coupon must be used to buy a meat meal anywhere.

2. The card is not transferable. You must produce the card whenever you buy butter, margarine or meat or a meat meal. The seller will detach coupons.

3. You must spread your coupons over the full period of your leave and of your journey out and back. No fresh card will be issued to you unless the period of your leave or duty is extended. Should this be the case you must take this card with the document authorizing the extension of leave or duty to the Local Food Office, who will issue you an Emergency Card to cover the remainder of your leave or duty. This card ceases to be valid at the expiration of your leave or duty as indicated by the date entered opposite 5 above.

PENALTIES FOR MISUSE.—£100 or Six months' imprisonment, or both.

June 25th Monday - Under way at 8:30 a.m. with two British ships and a convoy of 12 cargo ships, speed about 10 knots;

looked as though it would be rough, but is nice instead. Have a civilian aboard, either marine artist or writer from Washington.

June 26th Tuesday - Passed two convoys on 12-4 a.m. watch, and another on the 4-8 a.m. If we don't have a sub attacking this convoy, it will be because their "hain't none" around, as it is some big convoy for only one destroyer and two 18-knot sloops. Joined in the evening by four more ships and four English torpedo-gunboats.

June 27th Wednesday - No excitement. At 12:30 a.m. passed another large convoy. Increased speed to 20 knots, and left convoy. Arrived at entrance to the much-praised river Shannon, Ireland, and met our convoy, a slow-speed tanker.

June 28th Thursday - At 1:30 p.m., passed one of our subs, the AL9; gave her the demand and rec'd the correct reply.

June 29th Friday - Left the convoy off Tucker Light at 1:45 a.m., speed 18 knots. Arrived Queenstown at 7:30 a.m. One of our new boats, #86, the Stevens, came in shortly after. Underway again at 11:30 a.m., arrived at Bere Haven at 6:30 p.m. Underway again at 7:30 with a cable ship, only a 7 knotter. Rec'd letter from Aunt Marg. and Belle.

June 30th Saturday - Calm. At sea.

July 1st Sunday - Left convoy at Eddystone Light at 10:00 a.m. Had target practice. Wrote Aunt Marg. and Belle. Wrote Vena and Roydie. Arr'd Queenstown at 9:00 p.m.

July 2nd Monday - No news. Rec'd Vena's letters. No allotment yet, after a year.

July 3rd Tuesday - No news.

July 4th Wednesday - No news. Stayed aboard.

July 5th Thursday - Wrote Vena and Roy Jr. Under way at 1:45 p.m., leaving only one of our boats in the harbor. Fairly rough, speed 15 to 20 knots to catch up.

July 6th Friday - Caught up with rest of escort about 6:00 a.m. About 11:00 a.m., rec'd wireless that convoy was 48 hours late, and for us to proceed to Bere Haven. Arrived Bere Haven at 5:30 p.m.

July 7th - Under way at 10:00 a.m. with seven other destroyers; speed until 2:00 p.m., 18 knots; from 2:00 to 6:30 p.m.,15 knots; from 6:30 until 8:00 p.m., 21 knots, until we met convoy of 34 ships (cargo boats) at 9:15 p.m.; and the Mickey took position of advance scout.

July 8th - At 8:15, sub got one British ship, the Moss. All hands saved by Jenkins.

July 9th - Convoy split up on the 8-12 watch - 10 of them with the Stevens, Stockton, Terry, Jenkins, and us. We turned back 20.5 knots, into heavy head seas.

July 10th - At 6:00 a.m., sighted a sub which did not answer our demand; but after we fired a couple of shots pretty close, she sent up the proper signal and turned out to be our own L2. Arrived Queenstown 9:00 a.m.

Rec'd Vena's letters of June 18th and 26th. Still have not rec'd any allotment, despite the fact that I haven't been paid since April 1st. Answered Vena's letters, enclosing 4 pictures of myself numbered 1-2-3-4. Also rec'd Paula's letter of June 23rd, asking for a picture; told Vena to give her one of first four.

July 11th - In port. Wrote Paula, Mame and Dick. Wrote Vena telling her to write Bureau of War Risk Insurance.

July 12th - In port. No news.

July 13th - Under way at 8:00 a.m. with the Terry and a British sloop, in scouting line. About 7:30 p.m., heard depth charges off to port, and soon sighted a troop convoy of 17 ships, escorted by destroyer and sloops.

A letter on bulletin board from Vice-Admiral Sims, complimenting us for successful destruction of the sub we dropped the 9 "ashcans" on, on May 5th.

July 14th Sunday - Rainy and foggy. Picked up a convoy (20 merchant ships) at 5:00 a.m. Rough and disagreeable.

July 15th - Dropped 4 charges on a wake but don't know about the sub. But about 200 large fish and countless small ones came up; and it was too bad. This was at 7:30 p.m., in a fog; we were advance scout.

Lewie Stier, Feinberg, and Roy Moore aboard the McCall

July 05tg - Snl d ne bnmvny wdrd knst; aut wd rnumedc tgdl uo, Ymc kdet tgd kYst nmd hmDrdst Yanut 0:// Y.l ., Ymc wltg tgd Tdrry, gdYcdc enr P uddnstnwm Yf 05 j mnts.

Wrntd VdmY Ymc Rnychd, sdmehmf 2 ogntns ne l ysdke $4-5 Ymc 6. Nn dxbltdl dmt.

July 06tg - Brrhvdc P uddnstnwm Yf 5:// Y.l . Rdb'c nmd kdttdr ernl VdmY, Ymc o Yodrs ernl Mr. Hdkkhj dr.

July 07tg - Wrntd VdmY Ymc Rnychd Yf Ny Ybj . Mlhbj dy's dkdbtrlb Yk f dYf g Ys g Yc l d nmtgd iul o enr tgd kYst twn wddj s; dvdrytghmf hs f dtthmf nkc Ymc aul .

July 08tg - Umedr w Yy Yf 7:// Y.l . wltg tgrddl l drbg Ymt sghos Ymc twn tr Ywkdrs; e Yrky f nnc wd Yfgdr.

July 1/ tg - Ldet bnmvny Yf Drhstnk Yf 7:// Y.l ., turmdc a Ybj Ymc l Ycd 1/ .4 j mnts tn P uddnstnwm- Yf wglhbg soddc wd clc snl d onumchmf, hme Yfrky gd Yvy sd Ys. Brrhvdc P uddnstnwm Yf 4:// o.l .

July 10st - Wrntd Mr. Hdkkhj dr. Umedr w Yy Yf 6:34 o.l . wltg Std- vdms, Rnw Ym, O Yukchmf Ymc Tdrry, soddc 07 j mnts. G Yfr wd Yfgdr.

July 11mc - Brrhvdc Yf Lhvdronnk 01:34 o.l . Umedrw Yy Yf 6:34 wltg s Yf d cdstrnydrs Ymc nmd sknno, Ymc 8 l drbg Ymt sghos Ymc 0 Yfl nrdc bruhsdr. Hd Yfc tg Yf nur bruhsdr S YmF hdf n w Ys sunj nee Ghrd Isk Ymc. Soddc Yanut 0/ j mnts. ·

July 12rc - Nd Yfky r Yf l dc ay nmd ne nur bnmvny hmenf Yanut 3:// Y.l . O Yssdc Ymd Y st-anume bnmvny Yf 2:// o.l ., 1/ l drbg Ymt sghos. Wrntd VdmY Ymc Rny Jr.

July 13tg - Vdry rnuf g. Nn mdws.

July 14tg - Ldet bnmvny Yf 01:04 Y.l ., soddc 04 j mnts. Whmc Ymc sd Ys stlkkgd Yvy aut nmnur pu Yftdr. Brrhvdc P uddnstnwm Yf 4://

U.S.S. McCall   Sept. 1918

POST CARD

CORRESPONDENCE   ADDRESS

The "Mickey" (McCall), U.S. Destroyer, taking
one over while on a convoy trip in the Bay of
Biscay, Sept. 1918. Picture taken from top of
after deck house, looking forward and showing
a shower bath on the way to all hands on the
bridge, and look-outs forward. L.R.Moore, Ch.Elec.McCall.

AMERICAN CONSULAR SERVICE.
Liverpool, England.

November 19, 1918.

Captain Hains, formerly commanding the torpedoed steamer MISSANABIE called at this Consulate to express appreciation of the action of the Commanding Officer, officers and personnel of the U S S McCALL and at my request later sent a letter which I have the pleasure to send in the original herewith.

Sincerely yours,

R.M.S. METHVEN,

7th November, 1918.
at Montreal.

H. Lee Washington, Esq.
U.S. Consul at Liverpool.

Dear Sir,

After my interview with you at Liverpool, on October 25th re loss of our R.M.S. MISSANABIE on September 9th, 1918, I regret I was so rushed at the end, that I hadn't an opportunity of writing this letter of greateful thanks, on behalf of myself and other eight members of the crew of the MISSANABIE, for the kindness extended to us whil'st on board the U.S. Destroyer McCALL.

I would ask you to place on record this expression of the heart-felt grattitude and appreciation of both myself and the said eight members of my crew, for all the goodness shown us by the Captain, Officers, and Personnel, of the McCALL. Not only from the fact of their having rescued us from the water in a small boat, at the imminent risk of their own lives, but for the kindly sympathy and good feeling extended to us while on board. Their whole desire being to insure our recouperation, and comfort during the time we were with them.

Again expressing our grattitude,

I am, Sir,

Very respectfully yours,

Commander W.P. Hains D.S.C.

(Late MISSANABIE
C.P.D.S. Ltd. Liverpool).

64

p.m., having passed the US Navy tanker Kanawha and 2 destroyers headed out. Wrote Vena and Roy Jr., rec'd Vena's letter of July 5th, also proofs of Roy Jr's. pictures.

July 26th (no entry)

July 27th - In port, no news. Went on to Dixie and looked over my accounts. Wrote Vena explaining them to her, telling her also about the address change.

July 28th - (no entry)

July 29th - No news.

July 30th - No news. Wrote Vena. Rec'd pay, 7£, or $33.35. Wrote Aunt Marg. and Belle, giving correction in form of address. Wrote Vena about getting $35.00 worth of War Savings Stamps for Roydie. Loaned Jim Cosgrove and Bailers each 10 shillings. Under way at 10:00 p.m. with the Paulding, fairly rough. We are over-crowded, with new men for training.

July 31st - Met a tramp steamer; manned guns and gave her demand, which she answered properly. Half hour later, met convoy of about 40 ships (cargo) and picked out one; and together with the Paulding, left convoy at 12:15 p.m. - seas calm.

August 1st - Arrived Queenstown with our convoy at 11:15 a.m. Rec'd a letter from Aunt Margaret.

August 2nd - Wrote Vena.

August 3,4,5 (no entry)

August 6th - Under way at 6:00 a.m. with four others and three British sloops. Very rough.

August 7th - Joined convoy of 24 merchant ships and one cruiser (British).

Aug. 30th, 1918 - New orders.

At day general quarters report to forward bridge signal flag hoists.
At all fire quarters, stop blower motor in #2 compartment.

At general quarters for real battle, also stop blower motor on way to regular station.

More Notes:

Abandon ship - Life rafts

#2 small: Moore, L.R. - Harrington - Friedman - Brockie - White, J.P. - Bizewski.
#3 small: Middleton - Corbett - Rehmer- Quaid - Rozan - Burke.
#4 small: White, E.P. - Ward - Pierce - Triplett - DuBarry - Garris.

Abandon ship - whaleboat - 2nd load - USS McCall

Moore, L.R., S2 - In charge
Brockie, N.S. - Comp (?) and Sig. Flags
White, J.P. - 2 Rifles and Ammun.
Bizewski, A. - 2 Water Breakers
Corbett, J., S3 - Medicine Chest
Rehmer, H. - Pass up Rations
Middleton, N. - Report Boat (?)
Cunard, J. - Running Lights
Rozan, J. - 2 Water Breakers
Burke, J. - 2 Boxes Rations

Nov. 15, 1918 - Rec'd one spare armature for blower motor in plain wooden box stored in engineer's store-room.

Nov. 19, 1918 - Emery wheel washed overboard during storm at sea.

Navy Ships

Pennsylvania	Dreadnaught	4-3 Gun-turrets 12-14 inch (about 20-5 inch)
Arizona	Dreadnaught	4-3 Gun-turrets 12-14 inch (about 20-5 inch)
Oklahoma	Dreadnaught	2-3 Gun-turrets 10-14 inch (about 20-5 inch)
Nevada	Dreadnaught	2-3 Gun-turrets 10-14 inch (about 20-5 inch)

Above have 2 masts and one stack.

Wyoming	Dreadnaught 6 2-gun turret 12-12 inch (about 5 inch)
Arkansas	Dreadnaught 6 2-gun turret 12-12 inch (about 5 inch)
New York	Dreadnaught 5 2-gun turret 10-14 inch (about 5 inch)
Texas	Dreadnaught 5 2-gun turret 10-14 inch (about 5 inch)
Delaware	Dreadnaught 5 2-gun turret 10-12 inch (about 5 inch)
North Dakota	Dreadnaught 5 2-gun turret 10-12 inch (about 5 inch)
Michigan	Dreadnaught 4 2-gun turret 8-12 inch (about 3 inch)
South Carolina	Dreadnaught 4 2-gun turret 8-12 inch (about 3 inch)

Above have 2 masts and 2 stacks.

Connecticut   Pre-Dreadnaught
                     4 12-inch, **8-8** gun cns   12-7 inch, and about
Kansas   20 3 inch guns.

Minnesota   Have 2 masts and 3 stacks.

Vermont   The New Hampshire being telescopic in

New Hampshire   appearance only.

Louisiana, West Virginia, New Jersey, Nebraska, Rhode Island, Georgia

     Pre-Dreadnaught
     4-12 inch, **8-8** inch, 16-6 inch, and __ 3 inch.
     Have 2 masts, 3 stacks and super imposed turrets.

Good books to have

Timbies Elements of Electricity $2.00

John Wiley & Sons, Inc
432 Forth Ave.
New York City

Clothing and Small Stores Drawn

7/12/17 -

2 Blankets $10.40

1 White B---- .25

1 Scrub Brush .67

1 Flat Cap .62

2 doz. Clothes Stops .16

1 Comb .12

2 Pr. Drawers .70

2 White Hats .66

2 Handkerchiefs .10

1 Jersey 2.40

2 White Jumpers 1.40

1 Pr. Leggings 1.00

1 Neckerchief 1.20

2 Blue Jumpers 8.80

2 Pr. Socks .30

2 Towels .70

2 Blue Trousers 12.00

2 White " 1.80

2 Undershirts .80

Carried over $46.48

3/23/18

2 Cap Devices $1.00

1 Rating Badge Chief Elec. .40

1 Service Stripe .05

Total to Date $47.93

May 24th

2 pr. Drawers .70

1 pr. Shoes 5.00

1 CPO Cap 2.00

3 Cap Covers .78

1 " Device .50

Total to Date $56.91

Navy Pay Received

Date Received		Date Sent to Vena	
7/20/17	$12.00	7/20/17	$10.00
10/3/17	$165.00	10/4/17	$150.00
10/10/17	$35.00	10/20/17	$30.00
		10/28/17 Store	$11.00
11/5/17	$33.00	11/7/17	$30.00
11/30/17	$64.00	11/30/17	$60.00

12/30/17 Took out $55.00 for allotment. Had $11.00 coming but was not here to draw. Note: $3.50 taken from my pay each month from and including November 1917.

3/11/18 Received £10 or $48.67

3/13/18 Sent by registered mail a check to Vena $45.00

4/4/18 Received £58 or $282.28

4/8/18 Sent by registered mail check #305 for $225.

For insurance $10,000 current pay $7.00

April 1, 1918 $50.00 Liberty Bond $5.00

End of Log.

A Letter Home

USS McCall -
At Sea Sept. 8, 1917

My Dear Wife
and Boy,

I'll start this letter now and probably be able to write a little each day, and hope it may be a long enough one to make up for the time it will be by the time you get it. I hope you got the postal I sent so you would have an idea; but you will certainly know by now that we are away.

We got away from NY Yard at 4:30 P.M. on the 7th of this month, and dropped anchor at Tompkinsville at the entrance of NY harbor, until 8:30 P.M. when we up anchor and in company with the armored cruiser Huntington, the destroyer Duncan and several big troop-laden transports, steamed out into a cold raw wind, and I had the 8:00-12:00 P.M. watch. I rec'd a short note from Papa, and a copy of my birth certificate, just before we left. We had to dye a white hat each, as no white clothing must be allowed to show on this trip.

Next morning (9/8/17) the sea was very rough, and by 4:00 P.M. it was quite a storm, and we almost stopped every time we hit a big wave; and during the night solid seas came over our forecastle, carrying away our range finder, a sea chest, and one of our signal flag lockers; and at about 10:00 P.M. I came off the bridge to go aft, and a solid sea chest-high yanked my feet off the bridge ladder and swung me out at arm's length. But one knows enough to take a good hold of things at such times, and I had a good grip on the hand rails, so the only thing I suffered was a good drenching from head to foot.

9/9/17 - Later, on the 10:00 to 4:00 A.M. watch, a solid sea came up and caved in our bridge wind shield, took several of those on the bridge off their feet, and almost washed our captain overboard; and the weight of it buckled a "tween-decks" stanchion in the ward room.

We were compelled to slow down, so that we were left behind, as to maintain the speed would have completely crippled us in a short time in that sea; as it is, our paint locker and chain locker are full of water; and coming on the deck of our compartment, flooding the lockers - but not enough got into mine to damage anything but a couple of writing pads; but I was lucky, as the lockers in the after end of the compartment had three to six buckets of water in them, which of course wasn't perfectly clean - so those fellows had to scrub their whole outfit, and some personal effects were ruined of course. This tablet I am writing on was one that got a little bit wet.

9/10/17 - It was calmed down considerably by 8:00 A.M., but a big after swell running, so we were speeded up and rejoined the convoy about 1:00 P.M.; but they were in any old order, and one of them, the Princess Irene, was still missing.

9/11/17 - About 2:00 A.M. it began to roll so you could hardly hold yourself in your bunk, and the anchor chains kept clanking so I couldn't get to sleep; but think we changed our course so that the seas were on our beam, as there was no sign of a storm in the morning except the heavy swell left by the other storm.

We ran alongside of and made fast to the Maumee (our supply ship) and took on oil and stores; as soon as we finished the Duncan also took oil and stores; of course we keep under way while taking them, about 4 knots speed. The Maumee is partially disabled with engine trouble and has hard work to keep up with the fleet. Weather pretty nice, but getting cooler nights.

9/12/17 - Nice weather still; evidently they decided to leave the Maumee behind, so we ran back to her and took all the oil and stores we could hold at 10:00 A.M. and we left her, giving orders from the Huntington that she (the Maumee) is to make the best of her way to the oiling rendezvous. We ran into a slight rain squall at 11:00 P.M.

9/13/17 - We caught up with the convoy during the early morning hours, and about 8:00 A.M. ran close to the Huntington, and her commander wanted to know if we had oil enough to go 1800 miles yet as he said that we would have to go that far before we can oil ship again; and our captain thought we could make it; but the captain of the Huntington thought we would need a tow line before we oiled ship, but we didn't take it although our captain admits it is a possibility, and issued an order that no water can be used for anything except cooking and dishwashing, as it takes fuel to make fresh water, so that meant we can't get a wash.

Heavy wind and rain squalls hit us about 10:00 P.M. so that it looked bad for a while; but it cleared and calmed down before midnight.

9/14/17 Friday - A pretty nice day, we will have been at sea just a week now. We changed formation to a single column, the Huntington leading the transports, and the Duncan out to the right of the head of the column, and the Mickey out to the left of the head of the column.

About 3:30 P.M. the Mallory cut loose with her guns for practice on a small spar the Huntington was towing, and she did pretty good. (The Mallory is one of the transports.) About dusk the ships started a zig-zag course until dark, when we came back to our true course.

9/15/17 - Up at 6 bells, 7:00 A.M., and all the convoy in sight and just reforming into columns after the morning zig-zag; we were probably excused from it owing to our shortage of fuel, as the Maumee must be about 300 miles astern by now. All the rest of the transport had their turns at target practice today, and I guess they can make it exciting for a sub if they see its periscope in time. We dogged the watches today so that for a week I'll have the 4:00-8:00 A.M. and 4:00-8:00 P.M. watches instead of the 8-12:00 A.M.

9/16/17 Sunday - I have done all this writing today, my dear, and it seems as though it is two months instead of two weeks since I saw you and Roydie, and I'll sure be glad to see you when I do get back; and I hope in the meantime that you are not worrying but are bearing up the way I know you can.

We expect to meet some of our foreign service destroyers tomorrow, and then we will know for sure if we are to go back tomorrow or to go on with them. We are practically certain that we are going to go back to the US and wait for another group of transports. I cannot tell you how many ships we are convoying, but they are carrying quite a respectable army division; and there may be another group following us for all we know.

We are almost used to going without water to wash in and we are getting to be a fine-looking bunch of men. I was fortunate that I shaved just the day before the shut-down on the water; and if we turn back tomorrow we might reach the Maumee in two or three days, so I'll be able to get a shave before I need it too bad.

We are out of meat, bread and potatoes, so guess we'll eat canned stuff for a few days now; so you can judge that we aren't going to live like kings.

U.S.S. MaCall   World War One;   Sept. 1918

9/17/17 Monday - Fairly good weather, with occasional wind and rain squalls. Huntington had her observation balloon up early, and in hauling it down during a squall had it looping the loop and diving this way and that; it hit her mainmast, and we heard that one of the observers is dangerously injured; and am afraid that it is true, if anything it is a miracle that they weren't both killed outright.

No sign of our relief destroyers up to midnight; and it was some black night, but the white caps on the waves which were quite heavy by then were one mass of phosphorescent light, making it impossible to see more than three hundred yards away.

9/18/17 Tuesday - At about 8:00 A.M. we made out a large tramp steamer coming quite close, and we rec'd a signal from the Huntington to investigate her, so we put up a signal, "Heave to, or take the consequences," and she very promptly hove to, and turned out to be a British tramp steamer, bound for some port in Maine; she was loaded with sand for ballast. Her name was the Renwood, and she looked like a new ship.

We had not finished questioning her when several clouds of black smoke were noticed on the horizon; and they very soon resolved themselves into six good old US torpedo boat destroyers, coming at about a twenty knot clip from all sides. And just as soon as they had surrounded our convoy, we (the Huntington, Duncan and Mickey) turned about to buck a heavy ground swell as a starter for our return trip.

We will not get very far, though, before the good old Huntington will be towing us; and then we suffer, as it is bad enough to be driven through the rough water by your own engines; but it is a great deal worse to be yanked through by a big armored cruiser.

The seas are getting rougher now, and am afraid we are going to have some rough weather for tomorrow - and the smoothest seas on the whole trip nearly throw us out of our bunks in this little ship, and we are the smallest in our gang. The Duncan being a 1,000 tonner will most likely be able to get to the Maumee under her own power; we only displace 950 tons, consequently are smaller in every way.

We have had hard tack for one meal now, and flapjacks and biscuits and cornbread most of the time; but I like the hard tack, and hope we will run out of flour so we can have the hard tack.

9/19/17 Wednesday - Very rough, but sunny skies. The Huntington makes a pretty picture to us as first she shows part of her keel forward, and then smothers her bows down into the next wave;

and we are still running under our own power, but have only oil enough to last until 8:00 A.M. tomorrow; and we don't expect to sight the Maumee before Friday and probably Saturday, so guess we will sure dance on a tow line before then.

Well, my darlings, I am thinking of you always, but will have to stop writing now until tomorrow; it's too rough.

Well, my dear, this is continued from Wednesday the 19th, and I don't know how long I'll be able to continue, as I am writing this with my back against one stanchion and my knee against another, by the light of two wax candles.

When I went on deck Wednesday after writing as long as I could, then I found they were rigging the towing gear, and by 11:00 A.M. we were secured to one end of a steel hawser and the armored cruiser Huntington was secured to the business end of it, and towing or yanking us at about seven knots speed into a huge never-ending ground swell - and poor old Mickey will have her nose twisted off, as we don't expect to reach the Maumee until Saturday or even Sunday.

We shut down the generators and have no light or blowers on as we are saving fuel in case we run into too rough weather for towing, or sight a submarine, we can cut off and be good for about eight hours running under our own power.

Thursday 9/20/17 - Getting rougher all the time, and threatening rain squalls; so that it begins to look as if all the elements had been waiting to give the Mickey a rough time; for on an average we have had no real smooth weather, the smooth days being smooth only by comparison with the rougher ones.

We rec'd a message from the Huntington saying that her wireless had intercepted a message from the steamship Cryptic saying that she (the Cryptic) had sighted a submarine in the very spot where we were relieved by six of our foreign service destroyers. The Cryptic saw the sub Wednesday and we turned our transports...

(Time... I just lost my brace and had to scramble for my writing materials, also for myself besides. The stool went out from under me, the table edge hit me in the breadbasket (I mean hard tack basket), and I nearly singed my eyebrows in the candles, all because we hit some extra rough seas.)

...Tuesday, so you can see the sub was either a day late, or else was there and didn't care to risk the guns of eight fast torpedo boat destroyers, and the Huntington's six-inch and eight-inch batteries - not to speak of the guns on the transports themselves, and they are well armed.

It is calming down towards evening, but looks like some more wind and rain off to port, so don't have much hopes for tomorrow.

Friday 9/21/17 - It is rougher alright; the door of our dish locker just flew open and shot two dishes of butter, two pitchers of molasses, a bowl of sugar, and pepper, salt and vinegar all over the deck - and I came near joining the crowd, and it is some mixture. No water to wash with yet, and we are some rough looking bunch.

9/22/17 - Went on watch at 4:00 A.M. and the seas were running higher and the wind getting even stronger. About 6:30 A.M. the Huntington sighted a ship and sent the Duncan to investigate; and it turned out to be the much-longed-for Maumee, and about 11:00 A.M. she started oiling the Duncan and finished her about 2:30 P.M.

In the meantime we had got up steam and cast off from the Huntington's tow-line, and oiled slowly until 4:00 P.M. when an extra rough sea broke the hawser and we left, but were far from being filled up.

9/23/17 Sunday - About 8:00 A.M. were ordered to investigate a sailing vessel, which turned out to be a French fisherman; we had a French lad on board so soon were able to talk to him.

About 2:30 P.M. we were ordered back to the Maumee to fill up, she still having one engine disabled had dropped astern about twenty miles. We soon finished oiling and by 11:00 P.M. had re-joined the Huntington and Duncan, having left the Maumee, her orders to return to her station where she is evidently waiting to oil the next convoy's torpedo boats. Still no water to wash in.

9/24/17 Monday - Still rough; about noon we sighted the smoke of several ships over the horizon, and believe them to be the other convoy referred to. If so, the Maumee will just about have time to get back on her station.

I think of you both, my dear, every day, and during my night watches, and fully realize that yours is the greater sacrifice, as you know not where I may be while I have a very good knowl-edge that you are as safe as ever; and I hope that your trust in God remains strong enough to help you, dear; and you must not forget that one does not go from this world a minute ahead of one's pre-destined time - so I am as safe here as anywhere and hope you will learn to look at it that way, as you will be long hearing from me.

9/25/17 Tuesday - Still rough. We hope to make some port, pos-sibly New York or Boston, about Saturday or Sunday, which will be over three weeks at sea in very uncomfortable conditions - es-pecially as the Maumee had no fresh provisions to give us when we oiled from her.

They are going to serve us a quarter of a bucket of water today, and I hope it will get the dirt off my face and hands, after I first get a good tooth-wash out of it. Seas became a little less rough toward night. I do not say smooth, as I guess there ain't no such thing for the Mickey.

9/26/17 Wednesday - Was very smooth on the 12:00-4:00 A.M. watch, but just before 4:00 A.M. showed signs of roughing up, and at 6:00 A.M. was nearly thrown out of my bunk; and the rest of the time until 7:30 A.M. was just trying to hang on and sleep.

After breakfast, went up on deck and found we were just making speed enough for steerage way. The Huntington and Duncan made pretty sights for us, as we no doubt did for them.

9/27/17 Thursday - Calmed down and turned out to be a nice day; speeded up at 2:30 P.M. to 14 knots. A wireless message was picked up saying that a hurricane was headed up the coast.

9/28/17 Friday - Still fine weather, we must have missed the hurricane. About 8:00 A.M. a large steamer showed up in the distance and the Duncan was sent to investigate it; and it took quite a while, as the Duncan did not catch up with us again for a few hours.

They served us another quarter bucket of water, and I got a tooth-wash, shave and a bath out of it. Had a heavy head sea during night, but kept up a fifteen-knot speed.

9/29/17 Saturday - Had a very heavy wind and rain squall on the 12:00-4:00 A.M. watch and got wet through; but it turned out to be a nice day after all. We speeded up to about 17 knots just before noon, and they say we are sure going to Norfolk, Va. - and I am more than sorry, as we were so sure of going to New York and I was looking forward to seeing you; but we must grin and bear it.

9/30/17 Sunday - Had the 12:00-4:00 A.M. watch and as I think that we will get in before noon, I guess it is the last night for me on this trip. Could see land from the deck at about 7:30 A.M. and saw more ships under way at one time than I ever have before, mostly British and all outward bound, guess they will go across together under convoy of a few men-of-war.

Wrote you a short letter, dearest, to relieve your anxiety as soon as possible in case I cannot mail this one right away,

LeRoy Moore, Jr served with the Marines in China during World War II.

and hope you will understand when you get it that it is but the forerunner of a better one to come. My heart aches for you both, but you especially - as Roydie, thank God, cannot realize as fully as you do, so is the least sufferer of the two. Remember, my dear girl, that this trip but proves to you that there is little cause for worry in these trips for me; and I don't imagine we will be ready for another trip yet awhile, as the storms surely battered us some.

We are coming to dock now, and I hope we will soon be paid; and then I'll go ashore and send you yours; and if they do pay, then our accounts will surely be here so I can make my allotment to you.

I will close now, my own dear girl, and hope this letter comes as near as possible to making up for the delay. With my best regards to all, and my best love and kisses to yourself and our Boy, from your loving husband,

Roy

PS - I have never ceased to think of you, my own darling, and I hope and believe that my prayers have been answered and that you are both well and have some pleasure at times.

By the way, darling, did you write about money?

Roy

Form No. 213
Bu. Navigation
(Aug. 1918)

I issued VEC # 470 955
U.S. CITIZENSHIP CERTIFIED

Awarded Victory Medal with
clasp for Destroyer duty 11-16-20
Awarded Victory Button 4-9-20

UNITED STATES NAVAL RESERVE FORCE

DISCHARGE

This is to certify That No. unknown , Le Roy Moore

a Chief Electrician (G) (PA)(Conf) , this date has been discharged from the
Provisional or confirmed rating

U.S.S. 3rd Naval District and the U. S. Naval Reserve Force, Class 1B , by reason of

Expiration of enrollment

enter, Expiration of enlistment, special order of Navy Department (under age); physical disability; order Bureau of Navigation

(date); or other reason, giving same in detail.

Is recommended for reenrollment. Rating best qualified to fill, C.E (G) (PA) (Conf)
Provisional or confirmed rating

Dated this first day of July 1921, at Brooklyn, N.Y.

Active duty from 2-2-17 to 1-28-19

Lieut. , U.S.N.
By direction,

Commandant, 3rd Naval District,

Character of discharge HONORABLE

Enter in red ink "honorable,"
"good," "inaptitude,"
"undesirable"

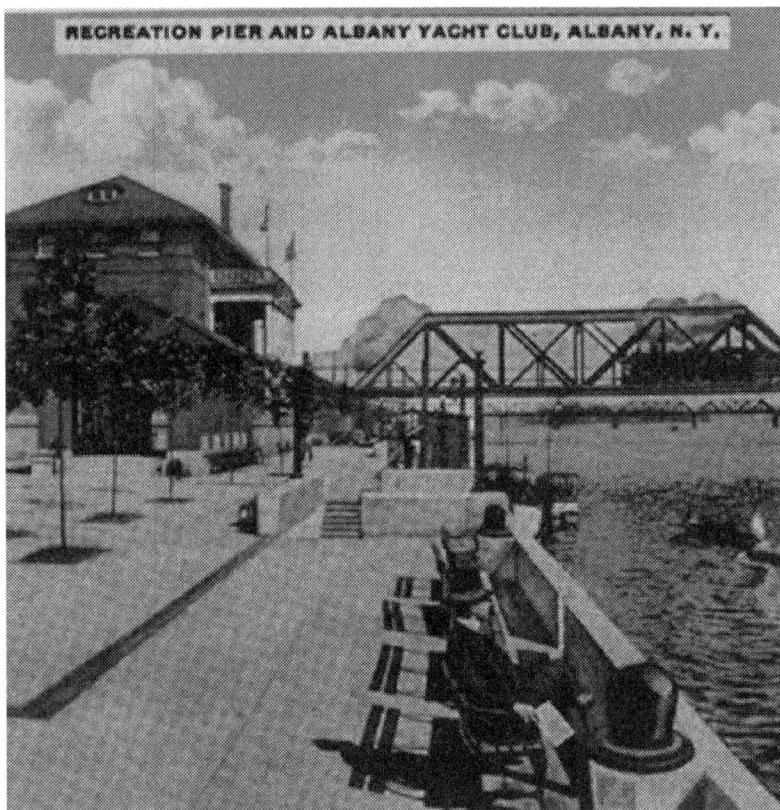

RECREATION PIER AND ALBANY YACHT CLUB, ALBANY, N. Y.

A Tall Tale?

Submitted to a
"Liars' Club"
contest at the
Albany Yacht Club
in 1939

by LRM, Sr.

Not being very good at story-telling, I was compelled to refer to a
rough log I kept of things that occurred during my service on the
old destroyer McCall. I came across what I consider to be the
most remarkable example of self-control and timing I have ever
observed.

Since this is a true story and the man in question may still be living, I shall refer to him only as "Spider," a nickname which he may have forgotten by now.

Anyone who has ever been seasick (and I have been myself, for two days straight) will more readily appreciate this story than those who keep their boats tied up to the floats.

Spider, being an ordinary seaman, stood his watch in the crow's nest on the mainmast. Seasickness was practically chronic with him, but it was noted that, while we had often to go to windward when passing the mainmast (preferring the clean salt water), when it was extremely rough he was never observed to "feed the fishes" - until on one occasion the McCall recovered from a severe roll rather suddenly, bringing the crow's nest out of the water rather quicker than any of us expected from such a roll. From my position hanging on to the weather life lines, I was astounded to see him - feeding the fishes.

Immediately after he came off watch, I sought him out to ask an explanation of it. He admitted that in real rough weather he had learned to time the McCall's rolls and was able to relieve himself while still under water; but on this occasion the ship recovered a little too quick for him, and he did not relieve himself until he was all of 3 feet above the surface of the water again.

Now, many persons to whom I have related this story did not seem to grasp the point of self-control that I am describing here, but seem to attach more importance to the fact that the McCall could roll her crow's nest under water. But to anyone who has been on the McCall a rolling of that kind was nothing at all. I have never been able to fully explain it, but on many an occasion the helmsman has been able on a severe roll, by a sudden twist of the wheel to cause the McCall to roll completely over and to come right side up much quicker than had she recovered in the ordinary way.

I might add that I have never had it satisfactorily explained to me why the McCall could be made to do this, except that probably from some previous strain there might have been some peculiar twist to her hull that gave her a slight spiral shape longitudinally. I offer this suggestion because I have never seen any other destroyer in the flotilla perform this feat, although it may have happened while I was still under water, before the McCall righted herself.

In conclusion, I wish to state that I am willing to be ruled out of this contest, since this is a liars' contest and I am merely relating this true story to point out that truth sometimes is stranger than fiction - fully realizing that in a liars' competition I could not compete with certain members of this club.

I thank you for your attention.

Request
Denied.

55 Swinton Street
Albany, New York
January 4, 1942

Commanding Officer
U.S. Naval Recruiting Station
Albany, New York

Sir:

I served in the Navy, 1908-12, as a landsman
electrician to and including electrician first
class. Received honorable discharge for same.
Served during the World War as an electrician
first class and chief electrician with permanent
appointment on the U.S. destroyer McCall, having
been granted a waiver because of 7½ pounds under-
weight. I am now 55 years old, have slight double
hernia which does not bother me in the least, and
I am still able to work.

I myself believe that I could still serve on a
destroyer, and would prefer such an assignment.
Since I realize that some of the foregoing conditions may render me of questionable value, I am
taking this means instead of a personal call,
believing it would take less of your time.

Kindly inform me if the Navy would consider me
under the above conditions. My two children are
grown and self-supporting, and I have only my wife
to support.

A self-addressed, stamped envelope is enclosed.
Hoping you will have time to acknowledge this letter
and advise me of your opinion, I am,

Sincerely,

LeRoy Moore, Sr.

LRM:jm
enc.

90

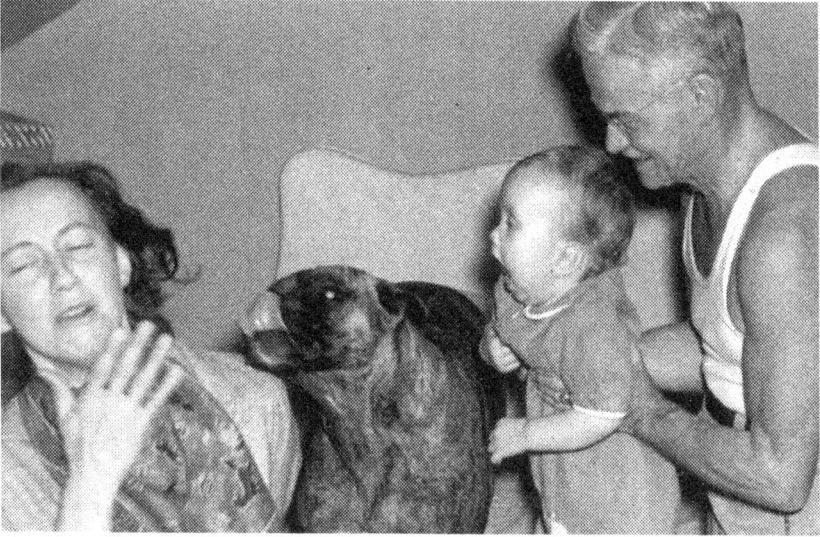

Jeanette, Penny (Uncle Roydie's boxer),
Stephanie, and Grampy Roy

A Granddaughter's Remembrance

Grampy had been ill most of my young life from the time I was born in 1954, someone to be quiet around, someone Grammy distracted me away from so I would not bother him too much (which of course made me even more curious about him). All I knew of his past was that he was a sailor amongst sailors, though he never said one salty word in front of his children or grandchild. He sailed with Teddy Roosevelt, well, sort of. And once, while on leave (and in his cups) had scaled the outside of the Eiffel Tower to its top. He was strong, slim, wiry. Not a tall man, although he always held himself like one.

He was very tall to me.

When I was three my Mom gave him a watercolor set 'from his granddaughter.' She asked him to paint his ship "The Mickey" for me much as he had done for her with her own crayons when she was little. Although he had never picked up a brush in his life, he

gave it a go. He painted ocean and cloud, fighting ships and wooden ships the likes of which have sailed our family's walls ever since. I don't remember him painting them. Perhaps he thought better of having his art supplies out while I was around.

By the time I was four, I remember him puffing on a pipe, sitting in a big red chair listening to the radio or records —sea chanties by a men's choir. "A roving, a roving, since rovin's been my rue I a. I'll go no more a'rovin' with you. fair maid." But

what I remember loving best was to go with him on his walks in the woods nearby. He even found an Indian arrowhead there once and I wanted to find one for myself, too!

One early and very wet spring he didn't want to go.

"It's too buggy out there today," he said.

What's a few bugs? I thought. I'd been looking forward to a walk all day. It was one of the few things we really DID together. What else would we do? I pouted. I pestered.

Finally he produced two pith helmets with mosquito netting hanging down from all around their brims. "We'll have to use these." He paused, "You're not going to like it."

What was not to like? I get to wear a big hat! I'll pretend we're going on safari! I tried to imitate a Tarzan yodel and thought better of it half way through. I could tell Grampy liked quiet better. It was a fine adventure striding down the street in our pith helmets like a couple of explorers, Remar and Professor Ogden, about to enter the jungle.

The first familiar stand of young trees was safe enough. But as we neared the denser underbrush a swarm of insects appeared from out of nowhere and enveloped us in a swirling, black cloud. My helmet's netting was instantly covered over with a swarm of writhing bugs just inches away from my face. I batted and swung but they were, they were everywhere! They were, they were ALL OVER ME!

I studied the rippled reflections in my cup, not wanting to admit to the debacle.

"No, too buggy." Grampy simply replied.

Why didn't he tell her how badly I had behaved to get my way? I chomped on a cookie and puzzled. 'Do what you like, but be prepared to pay for it.' That's what Grammy always liked to say. But Grampy had gone along with what I wanted even though HE didn't want to. Why?

He had let me make my own mistake, but he didn't let me do it alone. He had been proven right, but he wasn't taking any pleasure in it. But that's how it should be, shouldn't it?

Even when he wanted to be left alone, Grampy was good to be around. I'd always share with him what I was doing, even though he hated when I played nurse and wrapped my doll all up in wet toilet paper bandages. Even when he yelled at me "CONFOUND IT," or "FOR CHRISTMAS SAKE!" when the floor got wet, it

still felt good that Grampy was MY Grampy. I trusted him like you trust a climbing tree whose branches have never let you fall. That's how people should be, shouldn't they?

As I grew up this was the most I would remember first hand. Yet even now, all it takes is a whiff of pipe smoke, or the sound of a sea chanty, and I'm four years old again begging my 'Sail'rman Grampy' to go for a walk.

– Stephanie Ann Wiltse

Index

www.ingramcontent.com/pod-product-compliance
Lightning Source LLC
Chambersburg PA
CBHW031857090426
42741CB00005B/534